*The*
# NORTHERN
# IMAGINATION

# *The* NORTHERN IMAGINATION
A Study of Northern Canadian Literature

Allison Mitcham

PENUMBRA PRESS, 1983

© Allison Mitcham and Penumbra Press, 1983

Illustrations by Carl Schaefer

Published by PENUMBRA PRESS, P.O. Box 340, Moonbeam, Ontario POL IVO. Printed in Canada by Ampersand. The type is 11 pt. Garamond by Speed River Graphics and the stock is Zephyr.

ISBN 0 920806 46 5 cloth
     0 920806 47 3 paper

## CONTENTS

| | | |
|---|---|---|
| CHAPTER I | Introduction | 9 |
| CHAPTER II | Northern Utopia | 17 |
| CHAPTER III | The Wild Creatures, The Native People, And Us | 23 |
| CHAPTER IV | Northern Mission: Priest, Parson And Prophet In The North | 33 |
| CHAPTER V | Northern Towns — In Contrast And In Conflict With The Land | 43 |
| CHAPTER VI | The Violence Of Isolation | 53 |
| CHAPTER VII | In Search Of North: Grove's Canadian Siberia | 65 |
| CHAPTER VIII | Gabrielle Roy's Northern Innocents | 75 |
| CHAPTER IX | Yves Thériault: The Conscience Of Contemporary Canada | 85 |
| CHAPTER X | Margaret Atwood: Woman In The North | 95 |
| INDEX | | 101 |

ACKNOWLEDGEMENT

I wish to thank the Université de Moncton for its support.

Early drafts of some of the material published in this book have appeared in: *Canadian Literature, Canadian Fiction Magazine, The Humanities Review, Laurentian University Review, Boreal, Copperfield, Alternatives.*

*for Peter*

I

INTRODUCTION

Perhaps the most exciting creative force in contemporary Canadian fiction — French and English — is the Northern Imagination. Increasingly, our most perceptive novelists have shown that the Canadian imagination in many of its most original flights is inspired by the North. André Langevin's *L'Elan d' Amérique* (1972); Margaret Atwood's *Surfacing* (1972); Yves Thériault's *Agaguk* (1961), *Ashini* (1961), *Tayaout, fils d' Agaguk* (1971), and *N'Tsuk* (1971); Gabrielle Roy's *La montagne secrète* (1961) and *La rivière sans repos* (1970); Robert Kroetsch's *Gone Indian* (1973) and Harold Horwood's *White Eskimo* (1972) attest to the truth of this statement.[1]

The Northern awareness, however, is not quite so sudden or so recent as this list would suggest. Particularly in French Canada the northern wilderness has long symbolized escape from dreary settlements and conventional responsiblilties. Thus in French Canada a myth has grown up around the 'bûcheron' and the 'voyageur' and their exploits in 'le pays d'en haut'.[2] In English Canada the North has been much less the matter of myth and legend, and consequently a less common fictional theme. Only recently indeed has it begun to impinge deeply on the English-Canadian consciousness. Of the novelists in English Canada it was Frederick Philip Grove — not after all a Canadian by birth or education — who was one of the first to feel overwhelmingly the enchantment of the northern spirit and to evoke it in his work. Although his 'North' is most frequently southern Saskatchewan, he envisioned it quite rightly as northern frontier wilderness.[3] Indeed Grove found that Canada, as Siberia had earlier, appealed to him emotionally and imaginatively because its northern rigors were, for him, creatively inspiring. Since Grove, writers with as little in common fundamentally as Hugh MacLennan, Brian Moore and Robertson Davies have echoed Grove's comments about Canada's northern essence and resemblance to Siberia. They have come to see all Canada as Northern.[4]

It is, however, the far North — the still vast and deserted wild places — which increasingly dominates the Canadian literary imagination. It is the last vast North American frontier which presents challenges of all sorts and consequently conflicts of all sorts. In realizing this our novelists have begun to chart the psychological implications of the conflicts posed by the North for individual human beings. The northern environment with its rarefied atmosphere — Gabrielle Roy's paradoxical 'pure terrible country' — is the exceptionally dramatic background for the age-old conflicts between the material and the spiritual, between the dream and the nightmare, between wilderness freedom and settlement security, between primitive native and civilized intruder. Most of the dominant and recurring themes in contemporary Canadian fiction indeed — particularly flights, isolation and violence — are played out most successfully in the northern wilderness setting.

The northern exodus is astonishing in its diversity of questing humanity. Priest (Langevin's Dupas in *Le Temps des hommes* (1956) and parson (Horwood's Mr. Koch in *White Eskimo*), prospector (Roy's Gédéon in *La montagne secrète*) and prophet (Thériault's Tayaout in *Tayaout, fils d' Agaguk*), trapper (Horwood's Gillingham in *White Eskimo*) and artist (Roy's Pierre in *La montagne secrète*), lover (Thériault's Agaguk in *Agaguk*) and child (Buell's 'kid' in *Four Days* — 1963), doctor (Kreisel's Dr. Theodore Stappler in *The Betrayal* — 1964) and entrepreneur (Langevin's Mr. Peabody in *L'Elan d' Amérique*) flee northward to the wilderness. Even Kroetsch's graduate student in *Gone Indian* flees northward — to northern Alberta — hoping like the legendary Grey Owl to slough off his civilized veneer by becoming Indian. But few have the inner resources and the experience to cope with the isolation and terror of the North. The majority, after violent physical or mental conflict, either perish or return to civilization. All those who are well-attuned to the northern wilderness, or at least sufficiently disenchanted with contemporary urban civilization — Horwood's Gillingham, Thériault's Tayaout, N'Tsuk, Iriook and Agaguk, Langevin's Antoine, and to some extent Atwood's protagonist in *Surfacing* and Kroetsch's Jeremy Sadness — react against what the writers see as the sophistries of the civilized world.

Roy, Horwood, Thériault, Atwood and Langevin all question industrial progress and contemporary materialistic values — particularly the intrusion of Southern, though chiefly American, values of the North. Langevin's complaints[6] about the replacing of 'real men' with mechanical American-inspired inventions such as 'timberjacks', which devastate the woods by clear-cutting, typifies the protests made by all these writers. Their preoccupation with conservation — "And if the wolves exist, it is because mother nature has given them a role to play"[7] — and with the unmaterialistic regenerative potential of the vast northern wilderness dominates the contemporary Canadian literary imagination, distinguishing it from that of other countries.

If this aspect of the contemporary Canadian literary imagination has few parallels in the contemporary literary world elsewhere, comparisons with the nineteenth century American transcendentalists, Emerson and Thoreau, can hardly be overlooked. Thoreauvian echoes dominate: the stress on returning to a simpler way of life — particularly to a cabin in the woods, a preoccupation with the symbolic significance of the Indian (and by extension the Eskimo too) because of his ability to establish a balanced relationship and his natural environment, a distrust of the machine and the fear of the general debilitating effect of the encroachment of civilization, a poetic and almost religious belief in the relationship between the pine, the moose and the man, and an overwhelming faith in the therapeutic value of the 'barks' and 'tonics' of the northern wilderness as a cure for the ills of civilization. Indeed, most of the writers on this theme hold to Thoreau's statement: "In civilization, as in a southern latitude, man degenerates at length, and yields to the incursion of more northern tribes."[8] Among those who over the years have adhered to these Thoreauvian tenets are Catherine Parr Traill (*Canadian Crusoes* — 1853); Frederick Philip Grove (*A Search for America* — 1927, *In Search of Myself* — 1946, *Settlers of the Marsh* — 1925, and *The Turn of the Year* — 1923); Grey Owl (*Pilgrims of the Wild* — 1935 and *Tales of an Empty Cabin* — 1936); Gabrielle Roy (*Le montagne secrète* — 1968 and *Alexandre Chenevert* — 1954); Ernest Buckler (*The Cruelest Month* — 1963); André Langevin (*Evadé de la nuit* — 1951 and *L'Elan d'Amérique* — 1972); Harry Bernard (*Les jours sont longs* — 1951); Margaret Atwood (*Surfacing* — 1973); Yves Thériault (Agaguk — 1961, *Tayaout, fils d'Agaguk* — 1971, *Ashini* — 1961, *Le ru d' Ikoué* — 1963); Robert Kroetsch (*Gone Indian* — 1973) and Harold Horwood (*White Eskimo* — 1973).

Linked with the strong awareness of the natural environment and man's relationship to it, which all the above writers show, is the consciousness of the significance of animals — wild animals, that is — in preserving the vitality of the Canadian North. The destruction of our wild animals, writers such as Thériault, Atwood, Langevin and Grey Owl preach, ultimately signals our own destruction, for without the wild life our northland indeed becomes the barren wilderness that so many urban dwellers have long, and hitherto falsely, considered it to be. Thus Grey Owl called the beavers the "beaver people" or "little Indians" and suggested that, in killing them, man murders his own better instincts and his longing for freedom.[9] Langevin makes a similar statement regarding the moose in *L'Elan d'Amérique* and Margaret Atwood calls the animals substitute people — Christ figures indeed, for they "die that we may live."[10]

Above all, Canadian novelists show that in the white land — the "innocent Northland,"[11] as Hugh MacLennan calls it — there is the alternative of purity or nothingness. The white land, they show, is not a land which tolerates hypocrisy, weakness or thoughtlessness, and for the bumbling and inept or for those who fail to acquire insight and vitality, to preserve intergity and achieve a return to innocence, the punishment may well be the annihilation of "a white death."[12]

FOOTNOTES

[1] Paralleling these works are such more or less factual accounts of northern living as Farley Mowat's *People of the Deer* (1952) and *Never Cry Wolf* (1963), Duncan Pryde's *Nunaga* (1971) and Lovat Dickson's *Wilderness Man: The Strange Story of Grey Owl* (1973). It is interesting to note that writers of both fact and fiction seem almost equally in thrall to the northern spirit, substantiating one another's observations.

[2] For a further discussion of this theme see Jack Warwick, *The Long Journey*, University of Toronto Press, Toronto, 1968.

[3] If one doubts Grove's assertion, one has only to refer to the introduction of Farley Mowat's *Tundra* (1973) where Mowat proclaims: "The climate of the northern prairies (the tundra) is not so very different from that of their southern counterparts. Winter is longer on the tundra but not a great deal colder than on the southern plains."

[4] "In winter this whole land (Canada) is like Siberia." Hugh MacLennan, *The Watch that Ends the Night* (New American Library of Canada, Toronto, 1959, p. 160). Monica Gall in Robertson Davies' *A Mixture of Frailties* (Macmillan, Toronto, 1958, p. 246) in Paris suddenly feels "sick with longing for the cold, clean remorseless land of her birth." Brian Mooore in *The Luck of Ginger Coffey* (McClelland and Stewart, Toronto, 1972, p. 5) announces: "But the people and the snows and the cold — that woman passing, her head tied up in a bubushka, feet in big bloothers of boots, and her dragging the child along behind her on a little sled — wasn't that the real Siberian stuff?"

[5] Gabrielle Roy, *La rivière sans repos* (Beauchemin, Montréal, 1971, p. 118) — 'le terrible pays pur'. Translation: *Windflower* (translated by Joyce Marshall, McClelland and Stewart, p. 2)

[6] See *L'Elan d'Amérique*, Cercle du Livre de France, Ottawa, 1972, p. 75.

[7] Ibid., p. 224 (Also Mowat's contention in *Never Cry Wolf* and Atwood's in *Surfacing* as well as in "Progressive Insanities of a Pioneer": "If he had known unstructured/ space is a deluge/ and stocked his log house-/ boat with all the animals/ even the wolves,/ he might have floated.").

8 Henry David Thoreau, *A Week on the Concord and Merrimack Rivers*, New American Library, New York, 1961, p. 57.
9 Lovat Dickson in *Wilderness Man* actually calls Grey Owl the Canadian Thoreau. Grey Owl himself makes frequent references to Emerson's essays in *Pilgrims of the Wild* and he dedicates one section of this book to Whitman's "I think I could turn and live with animals."
10 *Surfacing*, McClelland and Stewart, Toronto, 1972, p. 140.
11 *The Watch that Ends the Night*, p. 318. In the same vein, MacLennan also says: "This air had come down from the empty far north of spruce and frozen lakes where there were no people, it had come down from the germless, sinless land..." (p. 241).
12 André Langevin, *Le temps des hommes*, Cercle du Livre de France, Ottawa, 1956, p. 29 ('une mort blanche').

## II

## NORTHERN UTOPIA

Many contemporary Canadian novelists — French and English — have focused on the northern wilderness in the belief that it is what makes Canada distinctive and original. For novelists with styles and attitudes as diverse as Gabrielle Roy's and Margaret Atwood's, Claude Jasmin's and Harold Horwood's, Henry Kreisel's and Yves Thériault's the northern wilderness has become a dominant Canadian myth.

For all these novelists the northern wilderness is a place where men and women in flight from what they feel are the decadent and sterile values of the 'South' may seek a heightened self-awareness — perhaps ever perceptions so transcendental as to be termed 'salvation'. In their terms the 'South' frequently becomes not only the towns, cities and outposts of civilization in southern Canada or even the United States, but by implication all Western civilization. The North thus represents a vast and pure, though at the same time a terrible and cold, reservoir of enchantment, where the disenchanted individual can hope to escape from the false utopia in which he feels trapped. His choice, if he remains in the 'South' appears to be between a mechanistic, communal and soft 'brave new world' and a mechanistic, communal but humiliating brutal and ugly world approaching that of Orwell's *Nineteen Eighty-Four*. The North — a new utopia, as many seem to see it — stands out frequently in contemporary Canadian novels as perhaps the only place left, not only in Canada but in all the Western world, where man can yet pursue a personal dream — where he can hope to be individual.

The farther North they go, our novelists feel, the more likelihood there is of their protagonists fulfilling their dreams. Unfortunately for some, actual northward travels are impossible. Only in their imaginations, in recurring and sustaining fantasies of a cold pure land at the top of the world do they escape from the urban noise and squalor in which they are trapped. Thus Paul, the terrorist-protagonist of Jasmin's *Ethel et le terroriste* (1964) (translation,

*Ethel and the Terrorist*) who is an expatriate to the United States after his act of terrorism in Montreal, engages in a mental flight to the North Pole. If he could only get there, he feels, he would be able to purify and renew himself. Similarly, Pierrot, the small boy who is the protagonist of Langevin's *Une chaîne dans le parc* (1974) (translation, *Orphan Street*), takes imaginary trips with his friend Jane to the same pure country of ice floes to flee the sordidness and pollution of a Montreal slum.

Many, however, do in fact travel to the Far North. One of these is Pierre, Gabrielle Roy's artist-hero in *La montagne secrète* (1968) (translation, *The Hidden Mountain*), goes to Ungava Bay in pursuit of artistic truth; and it is there that he finds his inspiration, his magic mountain. Pierre's love of the North produces a magic glow in his work. Consequently, the expansive and genuine feelings behind his northern drawings stand out in contrast to the cramped and bleak feelings which seep from drawings such as those produced by Sinclair Ross's artist-minister Philip Bentley in *As for me and My House* (1941). Philip, in contrast to Pierre, has lost the capacity to dream, the imaginative quality so necessary to the artist, by being confined within the false-fronted limits of a series of Southern Canadian small towns such as Horizon.

Artistic imagination and fulfilment are again linked with the North as inspiration in Yves Thériault's *Tayaout, fils, d'Agaguk* (1971). Tayaout, an Eskimo boy inspired by visions of past Eskimo traditions, dreams of travelling alone northward, far beyond the present habitations of men — and of finding there the mystical lost stone of his people. When he does make the perilous northern journey and does find the stone, he dreams of forms which he must extract from this special stone. In turn he tells other members of the tribe that they must consult their own dreams so as to perceive and bring out the individual soul dormant within each stone. Art thus becomes the province of every individual able to heighten his perceptions through meditation and exclusion of the materialistic values which rule the 'South'. All goes well until the tribe is betrayed into selling sculptures to a 'southern' trader and consequently betraying their dreams and their traditions.

Yves Thériault and Harold Horwood are the two contemporary Canadian novelists who are perhaps most convinced of the ideal or utopian aspects of the North. Both subscribe to the notion that the Northland is, as Horwood puts it, "such a splendid land — ... splendid like a country in a vision,"[1] and that the Eskimos are, potentially at least, "a nation of visionaries."[2] Heroic characters are the result of the authors subscribing to this thesis. Tayaout, Agaguk, and Gillingham are epic heroes — legendary figures who stand out in stark contrast to the usual non-heroes of contemporary western fiction. All three work toward achieving an ideal which is at once physical and spiritual. Physically, they are all of exceptional strength, with an ability to survive in the world's harshest climate. Spiritually, they are committed to an ideal: Tayaout and Gillingham to restoring to the Eskimo the past traditions which the white man, whether missionary or trader, has in his meddling intrusions into the Arctic almost succeeded in destroying; and Agaguk (and his family) to living a solitary Thoreauvian type of existence in a Walden wilder than anything Thoreau imagined even in the wilderness of the Maine woods. The magical aura which has surrounded the lives of Gillingham and Tayaout persists during their final disappearance and presumed death, and we are led to believe that, in much the same way as Saint-Exupéry's 'petite prince', they are endowed with immortality for those who sympathize with them.

The Eskimos alone among the peoples of the Western world have at their best, Thériault and Horwood maintain, an idea of excellence divorced from materialism. Thus if an ideal society is to exist anywhere they see the Far North — the North well beyond the greedy reaches and the endurance of the men from the South — as the land where dreams can be pursued and sometimes fulfilled, provided that the individual has extraordinary strength of body and of spirit. The land itself, the Arctic, moreover demands the preservation of such qualities as generosity, trust and loyalty as the price of survival: "If you live in the Arctic your life automatically is in your brother's keeping."[3] Affection and loyalty then are shown to be, ironically, much more in evidence in the Arctic than in any 'Christian' country paying lip service to such ideals because of the Eskimos' natural personal warmth and the fact that "the people they love are left free."[4]

Other Canadian novelists are also obsessed, though less

continuously, with the dream of a northern utopia. Kreisel's immigrant, Theodore Stappler in *The Betrayal* (1964), in his flight from the remembered horrors of Nazi Germany, finds Canada generally an "innocent country"[5] because it has been spared the mass betrayals and the gas ovens. However, it is only when he goes to the Arctic as a doctor that he finds peace and fulfilment: "... he found there, in the arctic wilderness, a kind of peace, and a sense of unity with elemental forces."[6] For Stappler, as for Dostoevsky's Raskolnikov, the northern experience is a healing one — an experience which dissipates his intellectual arrogance and endows him with the faith to commit himself to life. Like Gillingham and Tayaout, Stappler is at last mysteriously swallowed up by the strong and violent forces of the North.

The force which several of our novelists find in strongest opposition to the utopian northern dream is the American intrusion into Canada. It is this intrusion which particularly irritates Margaret Atwood in *Surfacing* and Gabrielle Roy in *La rivière sans repos* (translation, *Windflower*). According to both authors, American forays into Canada result in destruction of the natural environment and disruption of established patterns of life. The heron killed only to satisfy a crude blood lust and left hanging putridly from the tree on the portage represents for Atwood the destruction of Northern purity and innocence sacrificed to Southern lust and insensitivity. Roy's novel begins with the rape of Elsa, a gentle Eskimo girl, by an American G.I. during his brief stay at the Fort Chimo base. This rape is for Roy symbolic of a more general American rape of the North. Such a rape results in the birth of a new sort of individual who really belongs nowhere — a being out of tune with the traditional rhythms of the North. Despite the wilderness flights of the central characters in both Atwood's and Roy's novels, they remain unhappy and dissatisfied because they are too firmly caught in the nets of civilization to be able to escape permanently — to fulfil themselves in the wilderness as Tayaout, Gillingham and Stappler do.

Nevertheless the pattern of northward flight in pursuit of a utopian dream is clearly a dominant pattern in contemporary Canadian fiction.[7] The farther into the northern wilderness the characters go the more hope there seems to be of their dreams being fulfilled. Indeed all the novelists looked at in this chapter seem to agree that "this land gets better as you go north....."[8] Obviously then, according to our novelists, we would do well to learn from the North and from the Eskimo — and to learn our lessons well — before we destroy him and his environment, and thus perhaps our dreams of a northern utopia.

FOOTNOTES

[1] Harold Horwood, *White Eskimo*, Doubleday Canada Limited, Toronto, 1972, p. 59.
[2] Ibid., p. 67.
[3] Ibid., p. 174.
[4] Ibid., p. 72.
[5] Henry Kreisel, *The Betrayal*, McClelland and Stewart, Toronto, 1971, p. 34.
[6] Ibid., p. 216.
[7] Some other novels dealing with this theme are: André Langevin's *Evadé de la nuit* (1951) and *Le temps des hommes* (1956), Bertrand Vac's *Louise Genest* (1957), Ethel Wilson's *Swamp Angel* (1954), Roger Lemelin's *Pierre le magnifique* (1952), Robert Harlow's *Scann* (1972), Harry Bernard's *Les jours sont longs* (1951).
[8] *White Eskimo*, p. 130.

## III

## THE WILD CREATURES, THE NATIVE PEOPLE, AND US

As civilization pushes with unrelenting and maniacal speed into the last wild places on our continent — as the forest is bulldozed to make room for more highways, more supermarkets and more cell-like dwellings for the shoppers — it seems time to look again at the former guardians of this land, the Indians, the Eskimos and the wild creatures. The native people, of course, are now mostly like ourselves, confined and limited by what our tradition has pronounced best. They are the losers in what Gabrielle Roy has described as the basic struggle between the confining forces of civilization and the opportunities for freedom offered by the wilderness.[1]

Yet here and there Indian and Eskimo attitudes which we had thought submerged surface with surprising vitality and in surprising places, so that we are reminded of John Newlove's words in "The Pride":

> as the indians
> still ride the soil
> in us ... they
> become our true forbears,
> moulded
> by the same wind or rain,
> and in this land we
> are their people, come
> back to life

Thus it seems not unreasonable to wonder how much of our destiny has been — and will continue to be — shaped by them.

This current reawakening of interest is not merely the concern of poets like Newlove, but increasingly of our prose writers too. Consequently, it is the purpose of this chapter to reflect on some of the numerous contemporary probings in Canadian literature of the actions and attitudes of the indigenous inhabitants of this land, with the purpose of clarifying somewhat the relationships between these people and ourselves... and of charting their relationship and ours with the wild creatures who still inhabit our land.

The native people, those who still live close to the land, are not only our ancestors or "forbears" in the sense that John Newlove has used the new word, but are also, in the Thoreauvian[2] sense, emissaries from the wilderness and intermediaries between ourselves and the wild creatures who cannot make compromises with civilization or explanations to it. Because these creatures are uncompromisingly wild, we tend to forget that there is any link between their basic essences and our own. They become more than ever sacrifices to our lust for gain and to our increasing fear of the wild. Margaret Atwood has even called them "martyrs," stating bluntly that they "die that we may live, they are substitute people..."[3] and many other writers in both French and English Canada, from Grey Owl to Farley Mowat, André Langevin, Gabrielle Roy, Yves Thériault and Fred Bodsworth, have substantiated her point of view. Grey Owl, a Canadian Thoreau[4] one might argue, is perhaps the first of these writers whose basic thesis in his memorable books — *Men of the Last Frontier* (1931), *Pilgrims of the Wild* (1934), *Tales of an Empty Cabin* (1936), and *The Adventures of Sajo and Her Beaver People* (1935) — links the wild creatures to the Indians and, at last, to ourselves. He refers affectionately and intimately to the beavers as "beaver people" and "little Indians":

> The red men considered them (the beaver) as themselves and dignified their Little Talking Brother with the name of The Beaver People.... It would seem that by evolution or some other process these creatures have developed a degree of mental ability superior to that of any other living animal....[5]

Moreover beavers, according to Grey Owl, are not only intelligent, but provide countless lessons in love, gentleness and courage. On one occasion he says:

... with their almost child-like intimacies and murmurings of affection, their rollicking good fellowship with not only each other but ourselves, their keen awareness, their air of knowing what it was all about... they seemed to be almost like little folk from some other planet, whose language we could not yet quite understand. To kill such creatures seemed monstrous.[6]

Similarly, Mowat in *Never Cry Wolf* (1963) sees the wolves as related to the Eskimos and at last, when his wilderness lesson is complete, to himself, just as Pierre, Gabrielle Roy's wilderness man in *La montagne secrète* thinks of the caribou on the mountain as his brother, and Jacob Atook, the Indian in Fred Bodsworth's *The Sparrow's Fall* (1967), feels "that the three dying geese out there, which these alien hunters were not even going to attempt to revive, were part of his own pulse and life blood."[7] There are many instances in *Never Cry Wolf* in which Mowat brings out this point of view. We are told, for instance, that Ootek "considered himself to be magically related to all wolves"[8] and that Ootek said that "wolves have the same general outlook toward pups that Eskimos have toward children — which is to say that actual paternity does not count for much and there are no orphans as we use the term."[9]

That the Eskimo or Indian feels elevated by his special kinship with the wild creatures is a fact which the white man frequently finds difficult to understand. Langevin brings out this point in *L'Elan d'Amérique* (1972). Antoine tells the Indian that the visiting American hunters refer to him disparagingly as "the buck" — "the buck, as for the male moose."[10] However, the Indian is, to the white man's surprise, delighted! In one of his few verbalizations he says: "A buck! The King of the forest. You wouldn't expect me to be angry, would yoy Antoine? I'm delighted to be a buck...."[11]

Throughout our literature, authors realize that neither wild animals nor uncorrupted native people kill for sport. Killing for sport is another failing of so-called civilized man. One of the most disgusting instances of a civilized man's "murder" of animals is described in *L'Elan d'Amérique* when Mr. Peabody shoots one of a mated pair of moose from a low-flying cessna, specially hired for this brutal purpose. But there are many other examples too. It is hard, for instance, to forget the murdered heron hanging from a tree on the portage in Margaret Atwood's *Surfacing*, victimized by the visiting sportsmen.

The animals and the native people who are still in tune with their natural environment do not kill for fun. Even

> ... the wolf never kills for fun, which is probably one of the main differences distinguishing him from man (civilized man, that is.... This (hunting) is his business, his job, and once he has obtained enough meat for his own and his family's needs he prefers to spend the rest of his day resting, being sociable, or playing.[12]

Bodsworth makes the same point again and again. In *The Last of the Curlews* (1954) the farmer does not even pause before idly shooting the female of the mated pair of curlews, yet the hawk, which "could have killed the curlew with one grasp of its talons ... was a killer only when it needed food, and it gave ground willingly before a bird so maddened with the fire of the mating time."[13]

The animals are viewed by many of our writers as teachers capable of instructing even the white man, if only he will take time and keep quiet long enough to observe them and figure out their life patterns. Grey Owl, for instance, credits the beavers with his conversion from trapper to conservationist and upholder of the rights of the "beaver people" — those "small ambassadors from a hitherto unexplored realm."[14] And Mowat clearly wishes that he could find the same sort of felicity that George and Angeline, as he affectionately calls the mated wolves, have found:

> Angeline and George seemed as devoted a mated pair as one could hope to find. As far as I could tell they never quarreled, and the delight with which they greeted each other after even a short absence was obviously unfeigned....Wheras the phrase "till death us do part" is one of the most amusing mockeries in the nuptial arrangements of a large proportion of the human race, with wolves it is a simple fact.[15]

This is, according to both Bodsworth and Thériault, the Indian pattern too. In *The Strange One* Bodsworth's Indian heroine Kanina reflects on the life of her closest childhood friend who has clung to traditional Indian ways:

> Helen and her husband, she thought, were a team dependent on each other in a close and practical way that white people never knew. A white man with an incapable wife might be miserable but he could always carry on his job, for it rarely required a wife's help. But a "Mooskek-owak" hunter had to have a capable wife to complete himself, to make possible the full application of his own skills.[16]

Similarly in *N'tsuk* (1971) Thériault's Indian heroine announces:

> ...from that moment of complete awakening, I understood that Sholshe had a place in all my hours, not only as a male and a lover, but as a living presence.
> I felt the need of hearing his voice, of feeling his warm breath against my breast when he slept, of preparing his food and of healing his pain when he was sick.
> Now, it is easy for you, white woman, to love a man in your great houses, where everything serves you and you do not serve anything. It is easy to talk, but do your actions prove your speech?
> ...I could love in the sweat of exhaustion, throughout every pain, through any anguish; I could love in spite of all despairs, and even when a great tempest shook the country, and I risked death to accomplish the least task.[17]

For Thériault, Bodsworth, Grey Owl and Mowat, it is the stoicism and the passion of the wild creatures and of the native people in their natural environment which the white man would do well to emulate. Bodsworth's Eskimo curlew in *The Last of the Curlews* and his barnacle goose in *The Strange One* demonstrate both qualities frequently, thus making us aware of our own possibilities — and failings. In *The Strange One* the barnacle goose shapes the life of the protagonist, Rory Macdonald. In following the geese and watching particularly for the barnacle goose and eventually for his mate, Rory expands his perceptions and grows emotionally. Again, as is so often the case in our literature, it is the Indian, Kanina in this instance, who is the intermediary between the wild creatures and Rory. As Margaret Atwood writes: "The Indians did not own salvation but they had once known where it lived and their signs marked the sacred places, the places where you could learn the truth."[18] So it is that Joe Beaverskin (Kanina's father in Bodsworth's *The Strange One*) though a simple unlearned man,

> understood intimately one basic principle of life that most white men, shielded behind their artificial civilization, have long ago lost sight of. He saw himself clearly as an integral part of the natural world. In his way of life there was no confusing chain of time clocks, pay envelopes and grocery stores hiding the fact of man's real and ultimate dependence on the land.[19]

This conflict then, between the natural (the wild) and the artificial (the civilized) is basic to so much of our literature. Our authors, in true Thoreauvian fashion, opt for the barks and tonics of the wilderness. With the Indian as spokesman, the wild animal as example, their point of view is summarized by Thériault's Indian, Ashini, who describes the civilized white man as a being who thinks himself wise, but has never learned the only truly important knowledge — that of living.[20] "It is only we, the primitives, the savages of the world, who can dispense equity of judgement."[21] Thériault's reasoning here is again the point of view which we have seen emerging throughout this chapter from the work of writers as diverse as Bodsworth, Atwood, Grey Owl, Langevin and Roy concerning

> a people (the Indians) who have maintained, for thousands of years, the image of man before the instinctual forces of nature, who have travelled these forests as beneficent masters, without ever decimating the animal life, without ever setting fire to the trees,

without ever polluting the watersheds. Good masters, adapted to nature, who would not dream of disturbing its rhythms.[22]

Ashini and N'Tsuk are only two of the native prophets who have emerged larger than life from our literature. Indeed, our authors have almost exclusively assigned the role of prophet/seer/wise man to the native people, or to whites turned native. Among these are Thériault's Eskimo boy Tayaout in Thériault's *Tayaout, fils d'Agaguk*; Gabrielle Roy's Eskimo carver Thaddeus in *La rivière sans repos* and her wilderness man Pierre in *La montagne secrète*; Finn Schultz-Lorentzen's Eskimo leader Kumataajuak in *Arctic* (1976); Harold Horwood's "white Eskimo" Gillingham in *White Eskimo*; and Thomas York's "white Indian" in *Snowman* (1976).

Although the native people, as Thoreau also pointed out more than a century ago, are often, and with increasing frequency, corrupted by civilization, the wild animals, as long as they live, retain all their wild essence. These creatures become symbolic of all the wild essences which may still be ours. Whether beaver or heron, bear or moose, they are still powerful reminders of the wildness and freedom which continue to exist in this land; for, as Langevin points out, a certain amount of hope for strong and heroic human existence in this country can be derived from the survival of such an ancient and remarkable animal as the moose.[23]

FOOTNOTES

1. *La rivière sans repos*, Beauchemin, Montréal, 1971, p. 185. "C'est toute l'histoire de l'homme au fond, conclut Thaddeus, que ce choix trop difficile entre la vie au grand large, fiere et indomptable, ou avec les autres dans la cage." Translation: *Windflower*, McClelland and Stewart, Toronto, 1975, p. 54. "That's the whole story of man in essence," Thaddeus concluded, "just that too difficult choice between life in the great outdoors, proud and self-sufficient, or with the others, in the cage."
2. "Our ancestors were savages. The story of Romulus and Remus being suckled by a wolf is not a meaningless fable. The founders of every State which has risen to eminency have drawn their nourishment and vigor from a similar wild source. It was because the children of the Empire were not suckled by the wolf that they were conquered and displaced by the children of the Northern forests who were." Henry David Thoreau, "Walking," *Excursions*, Corinth Books, New York, p. 185.
3. *Surfacing*, p. 140.
4. Both write simply and poetically about the therapeutic effects of the Wild; both advocate conservation; both are preoccupied with the mystique of the North, the West, the Indian; both are avidly anti-materialistic and both stress the need for simplicity in daily living. Grey Owl's books are filled with statements which have a truly Thoreauvian ring: "A feeling of kinship for all the wild that had been growing on me for years, at this time seemed to have reached its culmination." (*Pilgrims of the Wild*, Macmillan, Toronto, 1935, p. 139) or "...but be it known to you that he who lives much alone within the portals of the temple of Nature learns to think, and deeply, of things which seldom come within the scope of ordinary life." ('The Tale of the Beaver People," *Men of the Last Frontier*, Macmillan, Toronto, 1931, p. 143.)
5. "Tale of the Beaver People," pp. 154 & 155.
6. *Pilgrims of the Wild*, p. 53.
7. *The Sparrow's Fall*, Signet Books, Scarborough, Ontario, 1967, p. 39.
8. *Never Cry Wolf*, Dell, New York, 1963, p. 105.
9. Ibid.

[10] *L'Elan d'Amérique*, p. 65.
[11] Ibid., p. 68.
[12] *Never Cry Wolf*, p. 145.
[13] *The Last of the Curlews*, McClelland & Stewart, Toronto, 1963, p. 27.
[14] *Pilgrims of the Wild*, p. 129.
[15] *Never Cry Wolf*, p. 67.
[16] *The Strange One*, McClelland & Stewart, Toronto, 1959, pp. 179 & 180.
[17] *N'Tsuk* (Les Editions de l'Actuelle, Ottawa, 1971, pp. 15 &16 — in French) or (Harvest House, Montreal, 1971, pp. 16 & 17 — in English, translated by Gwendolyn Moore)
[18] *Surfacing*, p. 145.
[19] *The Strange One*, pp. 197 & 198.
[20] "... a white man, who believes he knows it all, and has never learned the only science that matters, that of living." (*Ashini*, Harvest House, Montréal, 1975, p. 20 — translation by Gwendolyn Moore.) In French: Fides, Montreal, 1961, p. 28.
[21] Ibid. p. 45 (English translation) or p. 54 (French — Fides — edition).
[22] Ibid., p. 36 & 37 (English) or p. 44 (French).
[23] *L'Elan d'Amérique*, pp. 124 & 125.

## IV

## NORTHERN MISSION: PRIEST, PARSON AND PROPHET IN THE NORTH

The priest, the parson and the prophet march in the first ranks of northward-trekking heroes and non-heroes of contemporary Canadian fiction; and from the first it must be remarked that, as our novelists see things, the priest and the parson invariably have nothing in common with the prohpet. Priests and other clerics who are northward bound are shown generally to share the same frailties and lack of insight which mar their clerical counterparts who remain in so-called 'civilized' Southern communities[1] — that is, those who live in the ribbon of land stretching just above the 49th parallel. They are too often the sort Yves Thériault describes in *Antoine et sa montagne* (1969):

> The curé was absolute ruler of the elite of the village. He always made the first move, directing with assurance temporal as well as spiritual affairs. Sometimes, the law of averages intervening, he managed to be human and generous, but such instances were rare."[2] ... "Gently, but firmly, the influence of the people with money made itself felt and the curé accommodated his religion to the sauce for which they gave him the recipe.[3]

The northern clerics seem, for the most part, particularly out of place in the formidable and pure Northern Wilderness. The environment itself seems an antagonistic presence which is ready to chastise men who tend to be so hesitant, so worldly, so timid and so reluctant in their northward movement as these clerics. Somehow, Canadian novelists suggest, the northern environment demands men of sterner and more imaginative quality; not those who come weak-kneed from what they suggest is a decadent and stereotyped civilization, but those who themselves reflect some of the vitality and even wildness of their surroundings — and who, above all, love the northern environment.

The North, our writers show, does produce such vigorous and original individuals — and it is they, if one recognizes them, who emerge as the prophets and visionaries. These prophets are all either Indians or Eskimos or those who, through close association with the native people, have acquired some of their code and outlook. All break with sophisticated 'Southern' materialistic pursuits and espouse physical and spiritual quests which are closely allied to the natural wilderness environment of the North. Because they embody the Northern spirit, they are invariably, when they encounter it, in opposition to the Southern spirit which the missionaries have tried to foist off on the northern peoples.

Thus Yves Thériault's N'Tsuk, the heroic Eskimo woman whose courage and endurance, love and vitality, present to her people the ideal of northern values, says of the missionaries: "The missionaries have taught us many things that we did not know before — to steal, to lie, to abuse our bodies...."[4] And in Gabrielle Roy's "Les Satellites" (1971), old Isaac and Deborah, a woman who is dying of cancer, wonder why their white pastor, the Reverend Hugh Patterson, is so frightened of death and tries so hard to fight Deborah's death. When Deborah in her unsophisticated way asks why civilized people of the South try so hard to hang on to life once their time for death has come, the pastor is for the first time somewhat disconcerted. Still, though he wonders vaguely about the desire of civilized men to live ever longer, despite the fact that he has by and large not learned to be happy, the Reverend Patterson does not really conclude that the Eskimo has the best answer to death as well as to life. Thus he causes Deborah and her family to submit to the physical agony of a long-drawn-out attempted cure in the South. The cancer is not cured, so Deborah returns home, corrupted by 'Southern' materialism and having forgotten by this time how to die in true Eskimo fashion.

Similarly, Dupas, the priest in Langevin's *Le temps des hommes*, is well-meaning but hopelessly ineffectual. He flees to the north woods in hopes of finding a soul to save, and thus regaining his own feeling of vocation which he had lost earlier by the bed of a dying child. Dupas, however, does not save anyone — either physically or spiritually. Indeed, he is the witness to murder, and even indirectly, through his failure to intervene, its cause.

Another well-meaning, though blundering, northern cleric is the priest in Gabrielle Roy's *La montagne secrète*. Like the priest in "Les Satellites," he is of the South, not the North. Consequently, when he attempts to counsel northern spirits, he invariably gives the wrong advice because he lacks the northern imagination. Thus he tells Pierre, the artist-hero whose whole being is attuned to the North and whose inspiration is northern life, that he ought to return to civilization to study art. Pierre follows the priest's advice: he goes South and then on to Paris. There his spirit has been stifled by the civilized environment.

The clerics in these books have erred through lack of intuitive understanding. They are not all vindictive or malicious men. They mean well. Not so the missionary in Harold Horwood's *White Eskimo*. He is a man who believes in "enforcing Christianity at gun point."[5] He is one of many missionaries, Horwood says, who inflicted a cold inhuman version of Christianity on native peoples everywhere, one of those too who "turned worldly success, business, trade, into religious virtues."[6] Thus the mission became the focal point, Horwood shows, for a twofold robbery of the North — a spiritual robbery on one hand, and a material one on the other. Nevertheless, Horwood proclaims: "The Eskimos never gave up the warmth of their personal lives. They have always loved their wives and children and friends, and enjoyed the rich sensual life that the missionaries call original sin."[7]

It is Gillingham, something of a super-Eskimo (though white by birth) who sets himself up in opposition to Koch, the missionary, and who eventually breaks Koch's hold on the community. Gillingham, by his prophetic utterances and heroic leadership, re-establishes before his disappearance — Northward — a spiritual, unmaterialistic attitude among the native Eskimos of northern Labrador which will, it seems, enable them to live in the spirit which their demanding environment tells them they must.[8]

Whereas Gillingham becomes Eskimo, the protagonist of Robert Kroetsch's book *Gone Indian* acquires insight by turning Indian. An American graduate student, he travels North in pursuit of the Grey Owl myth as thesis material. On the way he learns to subscribe to the Emersonian tenet that "books are for the scholar's idle times."[9] He reasons, furthermore, that if a civilized Englishman — Grey

Owl — can become Indian, so can he. In the course of his adventures the protagonist, Jeremy Sadness, gains some measure of satisfaction through facing the northern environment. By winning a snowshoe race he asserts his right to be Indian — both in his own judgement and in that of a visiting Indian family. Still, because the Indian-as-winner is not part of the White myth, Sadness is punished by the white onlookers for winning. Beaten-up and left almost dead in the snow, he is rescued and restored through the ministrations of the Indian family. His experience — particularly the exhileration and physical strain of the race — has also provided Sadness with a brief transcendental awareness, a perception of being above and beyond the existence of his former self, the smart-talking graduate assistant from a Southern library.

However, the two most dedicated prophets of contemporary Canadian fiction, apart perhaps from Horwood's Gillingham, are Yves Thériault's prophetic primitives, Ashini the Indian and Tayaout the Eskimo. Both protagonists early in the novels which they dominate proclaim their separateness and their mission as prophets. Ashini sees himself in the role of savior of his people — an Indian Messiah:

> Then, like the Messiah of whom the white man speaks, I would go to preach in the villages, on the reserves, and to every group of turncoats among my people. I would show them this country, free and indeed their own, untouchable in perpetuity by any other than the descendants of the great Abenaki race.
>
> I would lead whole families back into these regions, and they would finally inhabit every turn of the valleys, every point of the lakes, and the banks of every river where fragrant flowers grow.[10]

And Tayaout announces in Whitmanesque fashion:

> I have been since the millenium ongoing man. I am without age because I am all ages. I am without ancestors because I am at once ancestor and future generations...."[11]

Even their names set them apart, foreshadowing their special mystical roles. Ashini, we are told, means "the rock"[12] — and he sees himself as the steadfast rock on which the faith of his people will be founded. Tayaout's name is called attention to in the frontispiece: "TAYAOUT, a name charged hereditary significance which goes back into the dark, timeless polar night: a name which evokes propitiatory incantations of shamans."

Both Tayaout and Ashini — and Gillingham, too for that matter — seek to lead their people to the promised land: it is a Northern land, as far as possible beyond the reaches of the Whites and contemporary civilization. The greatest problem for the visionaries is to wean their less imaginative brethren from the materialistic lures of civilization. This, Thériault shows, is an incredibly difficult task. No prophet in generations past, Thériault implies, has worked against such odds.

Ashini fails utterly, and, in a last effort to call attention to his mission, hangs himself from the wooden post at the entrance to the reservation where his tribe is caged. But even this action is misunderstood. Saints and martyrs, Thériault feels, are very much outside the patterns of contemporary thought and feeling, particularly in official circles. Thus, the official government death certificate reads: "Ashini, Montagnais, 63 years, suicide in a moment of mental alienation."[13] Like John the Savage in Huxley's *Brave New World* Ashini meets with no one who has not been conditioned or corrupted by the consumer society.

Tayaout is a more successful prophet than Ashini. For a time anyway he is able to capture the imagination of his tribe. He also goes farther North than Ashini in search of truth, and, as far as Thériault is concerned, this is the reason for his success, since this is where the deep reserves of truth lie. It is in the far North that he finds the two dominant realities and mysteries of his life, the mystical green stone of his ancestors and the great white bear. From the stone, his people, like their ancestors, are to carve figures according to their dream visions, figures which are not to be marketed because of their spiritual significance: "... selling these mythological figures, full of hidden meaning, will perhaps offend the goodness and the generosity of the gods...."[14] The white bear, it would seem, also appears as a mystical link between past and present: ("Was the bear a totem or taboo from the past charged with a specific mission?").[15]

Both the green stone and the white bear provoke dreams, and like the dreams which occur in the Old Testament, they are crucial to the lives of the contemporary dreamers. In connection with these dreams, Thériault feels that the Arctic environment itself is the necessary medium for the transmission of spiritual and supernatural messages: "Is there in this unvaried and mysterious Arctic some sort of unknown telephony sending out presages like news? Is there a current running like a flash through the ice and snow?"[16]

It is also important to Thériault's conception, that, apart from his individualistic heroic male figures, women generally are shown to possess and acknowledge intuitive and spiritual insights more frequently than men. At several crucial points throughout *Tayaout, fils d'Agaguk* it is the women of the tribe who, like the Greek chorus, are forewarned in dreams of various events and thus predict their occurrence: "...other women, Tiguk, Kriliak, Siksik and Arnaoyok, told him about similar dreams. In their own extrasensory world they too had been warned of an event."[17] And it is Iriook, Tayaout's mother, who, while talking to her husband Agaguk, makes predictions about the spiritual mission of their son: "The stone of the sea is divine: it has been given back to us and it is your son Tayaout who has been the instrument of the spirits."[18]

Although in the end Tayaout the prophet is killed and the tribe succumbs to its greediest instincts, the feeling nevertheless throughout the last part of the book is that the Eskimo, if he pursues his northern mission, will in the end endure and triumph. He will eventually escape from the greed and false values of the 'White' world: "The Whites have come and will go, but the Eskimos were there well before them and will remain there where, one day, Whites will no longer exist."[19]

Thus the North becomes a strategic site for physical and spiritual testing, and it appears that only Indians and Eskimos, or those who emulate them, can pass. They emerge as almost the only heroic characters in contemporary Canadian fiction. It is, our novelists suggest, their example that we must use to revitalize our worn-out civilization. It is they who emerge as the lay prophets of a new faith which has its roots in the natural environment. The novelists who subscribe to this notion are of the same mind as Thoreau when he preaches about the superiority of the native people in their uncorrupted state:

> We talk of civilizing the Indian, but that is not the name for his improvement. By the wary independence and aloofness of his dim forest life he preserves his intercourse with his native gods, and is admitted from time to time to a rare and peculair society with Nature. He has glances of starry recognition to which our salons are strangers.... The Indian's intercourse with Nature is such as admits of the greatest independence of each: the Indian does well to continue Indian."[20]

FOOTNOTES

1. Representatives of these Southern clerics are Philip Bentley in Sinclair Ross's *As for me and my House*, the minister who tries ineffectually to soothe the ninety-year-old Hagar Shipley in Margaret Laurence's *The Stone Angel*, the shadowy priests who hover persistently behind Grand-mère Antoinette and Jean-le-maigre in Marie-Claire Blais' *Une Saison dans la vie d'Emmanuel*, Parson Beamis and Dean Knapp in Robertson Davies' *A Mixture of Frailties*, Mr. Martell in Hugh MacLennan's *The Watch that Ends the Night*, and the priest in charge of the seminary in André Langevin's *Le Temps des hommes*.
2. *Antoine et sa montagne*, Editions du jour, Montréal, 1969, p. 48.
3. Ibid., p. 53.
4. *N'Tsuk* (p. 75 — in French) (p. 76 — in English).
5. *White Eskimo*, p. 86.
6. Ibid., p. 73
7. Ibid.
8. Theodore Stappler in Kreisel's *The Betrayal* is another white man with a mission who goes North to serve the people living there and who, like Gillingham, disappears while on a mission in their service.
9. Ralph Waldo Emerson, "The American Scholar."
10. *Ashini* (p. 18 — in French) (p. 19 — in English).
11. *Tayaout, fils d'Agaguk*, Les Editions de l'Actuelle, Montréal, 1971, p. 11.
12. *Ashini* (p. 18 — in French) ( p. 19 — in English).
13. Ibid. (p. 139 — in French) (p. 130 — in English).
14. *Tayaout, fils d'Agaguk*, p. 106.
15. Ibid., p. 31.
16. Ibid., p. 37.
17. Ibid.
18. Ibid., p. 114.
19. Ibid., p. 103.
20. *A Week on the Concord and Merrimack Rivers*, pp. 56 & 57.

V

## NORTHERN TOWNS — IN CONTRAST AND IN CONFLICT WITH THE LAND

Contemporary Canadian writers almost without exception have on one hand eulogized the beauty of the natural environment, and on the other hand deplored the ugliness of the structures man has imposed on the land in the form of towns and cities. The pervasive ugliness of these settlements, according to our authors is usually shown to justify at least partially the cramped and sterile attitudes which they find in the majority who inhabit them. With increasingly predictable and patterned regularity, our writers during the last forty years have evoked a series of dreary towns and villages which hug the American border and stretch from coast to coast. From Sinclair Ross's Horizon (*As for me and my House*) to André Langevin's Macklin (*Poussière sur la ville*: translation, *Dust over the City*) and Roch Carrier's village (*La Guerre, Yes, Sir!*), from Margaret Laurence's Manawanka (*The Stone Angel, The Diviners*) to Robertson Davies' Salterton (*A Mixture of Frailties, Leaven of Malice*); from Malcolm Lowry's Vancouver (*October Ferry to Gabriola*) to Yves Thériault's and Gabrielle Roy's Montréal (*Aaron, Amour au goût de mer* and *Bonheur d'occasion*: translation, *The Tin Flute, Alexander Chenevert*: translation, *The Cashier*) and Hugh MacLennan's Moncton (*The Watch that Ends the Night*) Canadian outposts of civilization are shown to substantiate Northrop Frye's claim in the "Conclusion" to *The Literary History of Canada* that "Canadian cities and villages express rather an arrogant abstraction, the conquest of nature by an intelligence that does not love it."

Now all this refers to the South (a Northerner's designation for southern Canada) — and, as most Canadians are inhabitants of the South, they have their own experiences in various towns and cities to consider when evaluating our authors' claims.

But what of the North? — our "unspoiled northland" as many still refer to the land above the 55th parallel? Relatively few visitors have been to the settlements or to the land which can be reached only by plane or on the once-a-year supply boat — a hardly surprising fact when one considers that it is still possible to be trapped by bad weather in villages such as Rankin Inlet or Pangnirtung for 5, 10, 15 days at a time beyond the length of one's intended stay — and at rates often triple those in the South — if accommodation is available! It is enough to deter all but the hardiest — and richest — individuals, or of course those bankrolled by a company or government, from venturing North.

Nevertheless, our writers — though still only a handful — have been North too. Again, as when depicting the South, they are struck by the astonishing disparity between the beauty of the land and the ugliness of the settlements. In the North, however, this disparity is very much more startling than in the South. It is particularly interesting that our writers speculate about this fact, because photographers in their beautiful picture book records of our northland are usually careful to avoid focusing on the settlements.

Finn Schultz-Lorentzen's description in *Arctic* typifies our writers' findings concerning the contrast between the natural environment and the settlements of the North:

> Daylight had come to stay. For two months not even a sliver of the Great Warmer would dip below the horizon. Goslings, cygnets, cubs and leverets would feed, sleep and grow. Heather would spread; saxifrage, green-tufted whiplash, yellow poppies, purplish bluebells come to bloom; cranberry, blueberry, blackberry ripen into succulence. This was the tundra white men called The Barrens.
>
> In the settlement, the advent of spring painted a different picture. Winter's waste, bared by the sun, littered the ground. With the clean rug of snow removed, the small community revealed itself as one vast dump.
>
> There were cans — plastic, tin, aluminum, any variety; sodden cardboard boxes; empty oil drums, crushed, flattened; bones, some still joined by half-chewed flesh; rags, papers of all sorts; the occasional dog, still in its fur, fangs bared in death. And amidst this general refuse, scattered in highly; visible desecration, discarded like

packsacks on a field of battle, bulked pemphigous plastic bags, their loads of human faeces ill contained behind loosely twisted ties.[1]

Not only does Schultz-Lorentzen depict the town as dirty — littered with 'honey bags' and other unspeakable debris — but as a place too where human relationships seem to be nearly always doomed — particularly those involving the Whites. Their relationships are invariably shown to be superficial, dishonest and crude. One has only to think of the hateful marriage between Peggy and Stu Spencer, both of whom are exposed as individuals totally lacking a capacity to love; or the affair between Ted, the mountie, and Sandra, the nurse, which culminates in Sandra's aborting their child because her pregnancy has frightened Ted; of the affair between the tough and dishonest newspaperwoman and the pilot who hates her but still wants to sleep with her.

The reader's horror of the White presence in the North and of the dishonest acts committed by bureaucratic power and status seekers there mounts until he feels that the individuals trapped within the grasp of this power — chiefly the Eskimos — suffer as much as the Siberian prisoners Solzhenitsyn introduces us to in *One Day in the Life of Ivan Denisovitch* (1963) or *The Gulag Archipelago* (1974). Although the means used to produce the horrifying state of affairs are not for the most part the same, the end results — the limiting of individual freedom, the suffering, the injustices — are not dissimilar.

And so it happens that the administrators rarely speak the Inuit tongue and are thus unable to communicate adequately with the people under their jurisdiction; that medical aid is often inadequate and tardy — as when Quimmiqjuak's and Suna's baby dies, and when Nigirq dies miserably before her file comes up for review so that permission is granted for her to travel South for psychiatric treatment; that the teachers come "to teach the Eskimos to be Whites";[2] that the press misrepresent northern events in which its members participate; that the travelling dentist views his patients as mere case histories for his research; and that visiting Whites steal from the Eskimos — as when a member of the press grabs the shaman's prized and priceless hand-made snow shovel from the shaman's house and thrusts a token dollar into the hand of the shocked Eskimo.

Above all the Whites are shown to be impatient and short-tempered — a state of mind which the Inuit simply do not understand, as they firmly believe that in all undertakings "good judgement requires inner harmony."[3] It is this temperamental difference between white and native people which is also reflected in Thomas York's *Snowman*, for it is as a result of White impatience that the Indian woman is shot from an airplane.

In *Snowman* York depicts the town, Yellowknife, as a blot on the landscape, dominated by the ugly highrise and even uglier mine as well as by the myriads of stereotyped government-employee houses, each of which was "indistinguishable from any other on the block."[4] In fact, the reader is told: "There were approximately twenty-five hundred such houses, twenty-five hundred civil servants in Yellowknife, roughly the same number of native households in the entire Territories; yet comparing Sommers' house to the houses at the village (the Indian village) — there was no comparison, except perhaps with the carport."[5]

Still it is important to remember that, except for the six weeks or so in the summer when the Indians and Eskimos can return to living on the land they are usually obliged to remain in the government-run towns which the bureaucrats have created for them.[6] Harold Horwood complains at length about this in *White Eskimo*. He states that the Eskimo is just not traditionally a town dweller. Moreover, Horwood argues that the Eskimo is particularly out of place in a northern community designed and administered by Whites from the South and abroad. He says of the Eskimos generally: "These people do not belong to a village, they belong to the whole land."[7] "... the village is still only a place to put up, like a hotel.... It was a shame, a crime, that they were ever collected together that way, and then drawn off, gradually to the south — farther and farther to the south — until the land out of which this people were born, the land of the seals and the caribou, the walrus and the white bear, was empty of men."[8]

In contrast to the villages, Horwood eulogizes the natural landscape: "This is such a splendid land — I mean really splendid, like a country in a vision."[9] Similarly, Yves Thériault's Agaguk refers to the tundra as "the pleasant and familiar country."[10] It is particularly noteworth that both these writers use a separate word for the far north. Their words "the land" or "the country" indicate their perceptions of an entity separate from the rest of Canada. Of course, it is not so surprising that Quebec writers, long used to speaking of Quebec as 'pays' should in turn refer to the vast northern stretches in such terms, but it is remarkable that Horwood and other Anglophones such as James Houston naturally adopt the same terminology. To do this seems a natural reaction since almost any norhtern traveller will soon find himself thinking of the North in terms of another country.

The visitor cannot help but feel almost at once that he has ventured into a unique place. The landscape is so visually different from most other places that he finds it necessary to adjust all the rules of perspective applicable elsewhere. At first distances seem impossible to estimate. A rock which appears to be perhaps half a mile away is in fact maybe four. A river, apparently just below in the valley, turns out to be three miles away. And so, like Alice in Wonderland, the newcomer to the North gradually learns to avoid measuring his northern experiences by the same guages he has used previously; and when he makes this discovery — or rather when it is thrust upon him — he experiences panic or a surge of exhileration ... perhaps both.

But to come back to the towns — here is what Gabrielle Roy has to say about Fort Renunciation in *La montagne secreète*:

> It consisted, at most, of twelve to fifteen cabins, among which two or three boasted a coat of paint: the company's post, naturally; the Sisters' tiny convent; the residence of some trader. The rest perched every which way on the outcropings of rock that emerged everywhere in gray patches, or else supported on piles in the mud, betokened complete human abjection.[11]

Roy's depiction of Fort Chimo in *La rivière sans repos* is even more desolate than this because it shares with other northern outposts such as Churchill and Frobisher Bay the dubious distinction of having had its development aided by the military.

Thériault's description of a bleak arctic village resembles Roy's and Schultz-Lorentzen's:

> It was a collection of a dozen grayish houses, with a few igloos on the edge. A radio antenna stuck up thirty meters in the air, a thin steel obelisk. At the entrance to the village, an enormous reservoir of heavy oil supplied heat to the houses, and near the Company warehouse a smaller building from which came crackling noises, sheltered a diesel electric generator. That was all.
>
> The monotony of these few buildings succeeded the desolation of the plain; they were no less desolate — in fact they made the desert seem more vast, they extended its boundaries.[12]

It seems particularly sad that the Eskimo, who was noted for his aesthetic sensibilities, should find himself surrounded by so much ugliness. In the past his own settlements were, by all accounts, often untidy, but without the soul and health destroying squalor which modern civilization has brought North.

Southerners have of course been quick to recognize the Eskimos' aesthetic contributions. 'Eskimo Art' has been popular for several decades. Both Yves Thériault and Mordecai Richler have done satiric sketches of unsophisticated Eskimos turning out 'art works' for greedy entrepreneurs. Richler in *The Incomparable Atuk* (1963) depicts a group of Baffin Island Eskimos brought South and virtually enslaved, joylessly turning out inferior carvings — far from their native environment which might have inspired them to do genuine and fulfilling work. Thériault in *Tayaout, fils d'Agaguk* suggests, like James Houston, that Eskimos are by nature and practice nearly all natural artists. Thériault, however, concludes in this novel that the Eskimos' creative instincts are ruined by the white man's interference in their lives — that they cannot and must not be tied to our materialistic system or the source of their creativity will be destroyed. Carvings such as those Thériault describes, which strive to bring to life the soul of the man or animal depicted, can be seen in the Eskimo museum at Churchill. Ironically, these carvings were for the most part done when life was much harder in the North than it is at present. They attest to the human and artistic vitality of traditional nomadic life prior to the existence of government-administered settlements.

In these new northern communities schools are important institutions, and, according to Roy and Thériault, destructive ones. Both authors, writing from the point of view of the native people, refer to the school as a prison. In Roy's *La rivière sans repos* the policeman is sent to bring Jimmy and his mother Elsa back to the community because the law states that Jimmy must go to school. It is this action which forces Elsa, Jimmy and old Uncle Ian further into the wilderness and precipitates tragedy because Jimmy falls ill and they are drawn by the need for medicine back to the community to stay.

In *N'Tsuk* Thériault states: "They are sent each morning to schools, as you call these prisons of the spirit where tradition is lost. When they are there what do you do? Can you live knowing that your children learn nothing about you or from you? How will they respect you later?"[13] Thériault's statement is substantiated by many observations in Boyce Richardson's study of northern native people, *James Bay* (1972).[14]

Such insights demonstrate that Canadian writers on northern themes are indignant about the plight of native people confined to ugly towns, imprisoned in institutions not of their own making, weaned away from traditional life on the land. Their indignation mounts when they see Southern developers as instigators of this Northern tragedy, concluding like Conrad in *Heart of Darkness* that "the conquest of the earth, which mostly means the taking it away from those who have a different complexion or slightly flatter noses than ourselves, is not a pretty thing when you look into it too much."

FOOTNOTES

1. Finn Schultz-Lorentzen, *Arctic*, McClelland & Stewart, Toronto, 1976, ppl 372 & 373.
2. Ibid., 133.
3. Ibid., 293.
4. Thomas York, *Snowman*, Doubleday Canada Limited, Toronto, 1976, p. 73.
5. Ibid., pp. 73 &74.
6. In only a few cases have Eskimos escaped from the towns. For example, on the Cumberland Sound in the Pangnirtung region of Baffin Island there is a group of Eskimos living their traditional way, led by a man reputed in Pangnirtung to be 'remarkable'. Similarly, hunters have told of meeting several Inuit families beyond Cambridge Bay who still lived 'on the land'.
7. *White Eskimo*, p. 132.
8. Ibid., p. 133.
9. Ibid., p. 59.
10. Yves Thériault, *Agaguk*, Les Editions de l'homme, Montréal, 1961, p. 11.
11. *La montagne secrète*, Librairie Beauchemin, Montréal, 1971, p. 117 (*The Hidden Mountain*, McClelland and Stewart, Toronto, 1962, p. 20 — translated by Harry Binsse).
12. *Agakuk*, p. 62 (In English; Ryerson Press, Toronto, 1963, p. 20 — translated by Miriam Chapin).
13. *N'Tuk*, p. 37 — in French (Translation - mine)
14. "Children brought up on the trap line become extremely self-reliant at an early age. From four or five years of age, small boys hunt birds and have their own special hunting bags for the animals they kill. They learn how to set rabbit snares and set traps near the camp for small game. They must take their share in the chores around camp, help their parents lay spruce bough floors and gather wood. They soon learn how to handle themselves in the bush, to recognize the tracks of animals and to gauge the strength of the ice they are crossing. By the time they go to school they have absorbed the cultural habits which make their adjustment to the grab-bang-and-slap aggressive world of the white child all the more difficult.

Suddenly children whose models of excellence have been their highly skilled but illiterate fathers have a different set of models held before them: business-men, office workers, suburban-dwellers and school teachers. When they return with the white man's manners, having lost their bush skills and attained some of the aggressiveness of their school chums, their parents are bewildered."

## VI

## THE VIOLENCE OF ISOLATION

In recent fiction of both French and English Canada isolation in the wilderness environment is a recurring theme, and, in novel after novel, the almost invariable result of isolation is shown to be violence. Whether the isolated area is North or West, exceedingly remote or merely on the fringes of an urban development, the novelists show their characters developing certain isolation syndromes — syndromes which usually erupt into violence. Emotions resulting from natural antipathies between characters, from jealousy, and from a character being forced to assess himself honestly for the first time are exaggerated by isolation and solitude. When this isolation is enforced by flight to an unfamiliar region, by environment factors like winter blizzards, or by unusual economic or social pressures such as a crime, unbearable frictions and frustrations result. Hitherto unsuspected criminal tendencies and violent actions often develop in people who previously have been considered stable.

This is a dark view of man's potential evil or susceptibility to evil influences which other writers have also emphasized. Both Melville and Conrad, for example, were concerned with the evil and violence which often erupt in alien and isolated environments. The peculiar atmosphere generated by the wilderness on exotic and remote islands or at sea, these authors show, increases the tensions and conflicts of men accustomed to civilization and is often the catalyst necessary to generate violent actions.

Canadian writers, both major and minor, who have dealt with the theme of violence — violence brought about by the frustrations of isolation — are legion. The violence is often provoked by physical isolation in an overpowering and seemingly hostile natural environment, but it is also occasioned by social isolation in an equally overpowering and hostile social environment. In both cases the frustrations of the outsider's predicament erupt in violence. This violence linked with the isolation is a dominant theme of such novels as Langevin's *Le temps des hommes*, Blais' *La belle bête* (translation: *Mad Shadows*), MacLennan's *The Watch that Ends the Night*, Ross' *The Well*, Buell's *Four Days*, Thériault's *Agaguk* and *La fille laide*, and Hébert's *Le torrent*.

*Le temps des hommes*, for instance, is a novel of violence dealing with the interwoven destinies of five men who are stranded by their occupation and the weather in a woods camp far from civilization. The nearest outpost is the dreary town of Scottsville. Situated at the edge of the wilderness, and consequently dominated by it, Scottsville exhibits all the stifling characteristics of so many small towns depicted in Canadian fiction.

In *Le temps des hommes* the five men who are forced to live in proximity are not compatible, and the awareness that they must put up with each other increases tensions and jealousies which already existed before they left town. Laurier's jealously of Gros Louis' success with his (Laurier's) wife is the most obvious source of violence, but there are other evident and increasing pressures. The obscene cook, Maurice, is obsessed with his failure to be liked by anyone, with sexual fantasies, and, as is finally apparent, with a desire for power and recognition. The 'Curé' experiences a sense of failure in his vocation which leads him to extreme actions in his desire to find himself through helping others. All these feelings exist in the characters before their isolation, but with the lack of privacy in the camp, long evenings idly spent, their need to depend on and trust each other, together with their inability to do so, the little idiosyncrasies of each man which irk the others, their nerves become more and more frayed. But it is the blizzard which acts as a powerful catalyst on their already touchy tempers. From the psychological effects of the blizzard violence is brought about and multiple murders are enacted. Indeed, the atmosphere is so charged that even the apparently impotent cook kills his man to show what he can do.

The influence here of the most extreme winter conditions cannot be underestimated. Indeed, in many Canadian novels, winter itself can almost be considered as a powerful and deadly character. In Buckler's *The Mountain and the Valley*, the hero, David, eventually perishes at the top of his mountain in the dead of winter, and Roy's Pierre in *La montagne secrète* comes close to death when caught on his mountain during the first winter blizzard. In Pellerin's *Un soir d'hiver* winter and death (murder) are again linked, and in both Langevin's *Evadé de la nuit* and McCourt's *Home is the Stranger* the search for death is closely associated with the blizzard.

Often it is the confining power of winter which in Canadian fiction forces emotional tensions to a breaking point. In *Agaguk*, for instance, the brutality of Agaguk's violence during the birth of his first child and his desire to murder his second child, a girl, can be at least partially attributed to the frustrations arising from long confinement within the igloo. Again in *Le temps des hommes* part of the violence is a reaction against the same sort of frustrating confinement during bitter winter conditions.

In *Agaguk* too Thériault stresses the human paralysis which is attendant on the northern winter:

> The cold was a mass resting on the surface of the earth, crushing all life out of living things. A pale light came from the south, but the north was dark. Up there was the six-month night, the terrible endless night of the Arctic, no wind, only the cold, all powerful presence, a cold in bluish colours, paralyzing all energy, inviting to fatal drowsiness.[1]

Similarly Roy's artist-hero, Pierre, experiences paralysis in the northern winter, but in addition winter is responsible for the death of creativity. Closed up and snowed in in a northern cabin, Pierre realizes that all he can hope for during the cruelest part of the winter is physical survival. However, almost defeated even in his attempt to maintain physical life due to an attack of scurvy, he finds that his soul has also suffered, and in place of his formerly intense creative drive is sterility. It is only in response to the first rays of spring sunshine that Pierre's creativity is revived.

By reasons of climate and primitive conditions long since past in the Old World, instances in most other literatures, except Russian, of the psychological effects of winter on fictional characters are fairly rare. D.H. Lawrence, however, one of the few British writers to concern himself with this subject, has one memorable winter interlude in *Women in Love*, but is obliged to remove his characters from England to Switzerland for the sequence of appropriate winter scenes. The effect of the indoor claustrophobic tension is outdoor violence in Lawrence's novel — very much as it is in the various Canadian novels mentioned. Indeed, Lawrence's snow scene, which involves attempted murder and suicide, is probably the most violent scene in any of his novels.

In much the same manner, certain instances of violence and passion in such masterpieces of Russian fiction as *War and Peace*, *Dr. Zhivago*, and *Crime and Punishment* have also to do with winter landscapes and with the problems and passions they generate. And although nineteenth century Canadians were infuriated by Voltaire's earlier dismissal of Canada as 'several acres of snow' and sophisticated twentieth century Canadians tend to laugh at the statement from their superheated city apartments, nevertheless, the literary impact on the Canadian writer of these 'acres of snow', where there is always the threat of 'a white death' cannot be denied.

Another aspect of the violence of solitude in Canadian literature is that developed by Anne Hébert in *Le torrent* and Marie-Claire Blais in *La belle bête*. The brutality and the torment are particularly dreadful here because the characters who are tortured most are children, completely helpless victims of solitude. In both novels, in fact, because the action takes place in the depths of the country where there is no stranger or neighbour to see or intervene, the cruelty and violence of the mothers to their children is unbounded. The psychological and physical cruelty inflicted on François, by his mother in *Le torrent*, for instance, is extensive. Until he is twelve François hears nothing but "words of punishment," "juctice of God," "Hell," "dicipline," "original sin." When he tries to run away it is only to meet an evil man who frightens him and from whom, ironically, he is suddenly violently delivered by his mother who makes a sudden appearance. After this episode his mother reminds him: "The world is not beautiful, François. You mustn't get involved in it....Do what you're asked to do, without looking around."[2] Flight, for François, has been prevented so now he is forced because he is a child to submit to his authoritarian mother, who, significantly, is herself a fugitive from society: in fact, it is from her own suffering as a fugitive that she has presumably grown so bitter. Lonely, frustrated and exiled, her most rancorous and violent impulses multiply. She sends François off to train as a priest, but his soul has been destroyed: "I did not know happiness. I could not know happiness....My heart was bitter, ravaged. I was seventeen."[3]

When he refuses to continue with his training she strikes him on the head, permanently deafening him. From then he is practically driven mad by an almost continuous roaring sound in his head which reminds him of the roaring of the waterfall near the house, the one that had had such an overpowering effect on him throughout his childhood and indeed up to the time of his deafness. Meanwhile, in total isolation now, François' hatred of his violent mother festers until a similar violence erupts in himself. He lets the stallion, Percival, loose expressly to kill her; the stallion here, as in Ross's *The Well* and indeed in D.H. Lawrence's *St. Mawr*, emphasizes through symbol the violence of the passions which have been unleashed. Indeed such violence and hatred frustrate all natural desires. When he takes the girl Amica home he finds himself not only sexually frigid but devoid of any tenderness whatsoever. As he says himself: "Brutality is the recourse of those who no longer have any inner resources."[4] His final act of violence occurs when he hurls himself into the torrent.

The mother-son relationship depicted in *Le torrent* is a situation parallel to the one developed in Hugh MacLennan's *The Watch that Ends the Night*. In MacLennan's novel there is again the wilderness and isolation and a woman whose frustration and inhumanity drive her young son, Jerome, to flight. Admittedly there is considerable difference in the details of the two situations. François and his mother in *Le torrent* are completely alone, whereas Jerome and his mother in MacLennan's novel live in an isolated lumber camp. The violence in MacLennan's novel, furthermore, is provoked by Jerome's mother who chooses one of the men to sleep with her and then taunts him for his sexual inadequacy, so it is the man who kills her for her taunts. In Hébert's novel the mother exudes such venom almost continually that the violent outcome is inevitable. Also, whereas Jerome's flight from isolation and violence is successful, François is not, and eventually Jerome fulfills himself as a brilliant doctor, whereas François' unsuccessful flight is the beginning of a steady spiritual and mental deterioration.

In Blais' *La belle bête* there is a similar sort of structure — horror built on horror, terror on terror. The mother hates her daughter and dotes on her son. Consequently, the daughter, Isabelle-Marie, becomes warped like François of *Le torrent*, and begins to inflict the sort of torture she had received from her mother on her half-witted brother who has been left to her care. Indeed, bit by bit, she nearly succeeds in starving him to death. There is, however, a tranquil interlude — a sort of pastoral idyll — when Isabelle-Marie finds a lover and flees her torment, but it is short-lived. Violence and evil erupt again after the flight when her lover, who has been blind, regains his sight and immediately rejects her and their baby girl because of their physical ugliness. Rejected by her lover and spurned by her family, Isabelle-Marie in a final act of vengeful violence burns the crops belonging to her mother whom she still blames for her basic unhappiness.

John Buell's *Four Days* is another novel concerned with a child's involvement in, and inability to cope with, patterns of flight and violence. In this case the child is a particularly intelligent and self-reliant boy who manages an escape, following a bank robbery and the subsequent violent death of his brother, with much the same sort of courage and resourcefulness which the boy, Jerome, shows in MacClennan's *The Watch that Ends the Night*. But unlike Jerome, Buell's boy is not so fortunate in the people he meets. The hotel clerk where he stays is not only suspicious of him but linked with small-time gangsters who plan to rob him. Fearful and unhappy but on his guard, the boy thinks that he can trust an attractive young man who has been kind to him, but his trust is misplaced. Alone with his new friend in a remote lakeside cottage the man reveals himself a homosexual. The boy's panic when he awakens to find the man caressing him is reminiscent of Holden Caulfield's in Salinger's *The Catcher in the Rye* when he flees from the caresses of Mr. Antolini. But Buell's boy cannot, like Holden, simply rush out of the apartment and jump into the elevator. For Buell's "kid" there appears no alternative to violence; therefore, he pulls out the knife given him for emergencies by his brother, and kills the man.

Sexual frustration combined with isolation is another suitable stimulant to violence. Ross' *The Well*, Thériault's *La fille laide* and Langevin's *Le temps des hommes* all deal with the love triangle. In

Thériault's story two women want the same man and in Ross' and Langevin's two men want the same woman. Because of isolation, proximity is enforced and the outcome is bloody.

In *The Well* the young man is a fugitive from the law, but the married woman has guessed this and has threatened to expose him; therefore, he feels trapped. The situation is complicated, moreover, by the fact that he finds her very attractive. Eventually, unable to withstand temptation, he sleeps with her, even though her husband is in another part of the house. It is the woman, however, who is driven to violence — not the young man. She shoots her aging husband out of lust for the young man it is true, but it is equally true that such a remedy is the final resort of a town girl driven to desperation by years on an isolated farm. The situation in Thériault's *La fille laide* is somewhat similar, and, in addition, there is also a similarity between it and MacLennan's *The Watch that Ends the Night*. Both have characaters, Bernadette and Jerome's mother respectively, who have enormous, brutal and completely selfish sexual appetites, and both are savage in their attempts to gratify these appetites. Bernadette, suspecting that Fabien loves Edith, 'la fille laide', feels sure that her own beauty will lure him away. When this fails, she threatens him. Fabien, already pushed to the psychological limits of endurance, kills her in a fit of passionate rage, an act which, like the violence in both Ross' and MacLennan's novels, is the outcome of sexual drives in women made desperate through isolation.

In *Le temps des hommes* Yolande is also made desperate by frustration increased by her isolation in the remote paper company town of Scottsville — the last outpost before the vast expanses of wilderness. Her inability to escape from the town and her unhappy marriage to the mean-spirited and insanely jealous Laurier drive her into the arms of the happy-go-lucky Gros Louis. This action goads Laurier into murderous violence which is inescapable because of the fact that Laurier and Gros Louis are cooped up together in an isolated woods camp.

Several of the murders in these novels, moreover, just as in *Agaguk*, presumably go unsolved by the authoritiesl In isolated circumstances there are usually no witnesses, no prying neighbors, no gossip, no opinions, only Nature, mute and impassive before

59

passionate but natural occurrences. Indeed, to survive in the wilderness at all, man must have quick reactions — a certain reliance on instinct to preserve himself physically and mentally.

There are numerous instances in Thériault's work of the need for controlled and calculated violence for preservation of individual liberty in the wilderness. One of the most striking examples is in *Agaguk* when Iriook, Agaguk's wife, calmly levels her gun at the crafty Ghorok to warn him that she will not tolerate his intrusion: "I know how to kill too."[5] Agaguk as well, both before and after his confrontation with the white wolf and his subsequent illness, needs to draw on this same reservoir of controlled violence in order to survive in his violent environment. He thrives on his awareness of his strength and his ability to survive and to conquer. This ability is a day-to-day measure of his virility. He has come to terms with his environment, and must pass on this ability to his son. Thus he can hardly wait to initiate Tayaout into the uses of violence in the wilderness — the tracking of other creatures, the use of knife and gun, and the savour of blood. This taste he inculcates by giving the infant Tayaout a fresh raw piece of rabbit, dripping blood, to suck.

It is only when Agaguk's violence becomes uncontrolled, unreasonable and unnaturally destructive that Nature herself seems to punish him by sending as the agent of retribution the 'Agiortok', the white wolf. Then the violence dominates and nearly destroys him. The hunter becomes the hunted — a theme which is so important in the work of D.H. Lawrence, in Melville's *Moby Dick* and also in the Langevin's *Le temps des hommes*. In *Le temps des hommes* when Laurier seeks refuge from the police in a brush shelter near the lake he realizes that his role in life has been reversed. Now as he cringes helpless he resembles the deer he had hunted in the past. Laurier's brutal murder of Gros Louis, like Agaguk's murder of Brown, has precipitated his flight into the violent world of nightmare fringing on madness which Thériault terms "this new nightmare country."

Agaguk escapes destruction and reaches a deeper comprehension of life and of his own role in it because of his ability to evolve and to change through experience. He acquires a heightened awareness of both Iriook and Nature. His creative instincts balance his destructive ones. In contrast, Laurier is doomed because he is too insensitive to change. Frustrated, a spoiled product of an inferior civilization, his instincts become destructive only.

Thériault's concern with letting in the wilderness, with having his characters Iriook and Agaguk come to terms with their environment, is paralled by W.O. Mitchell's similar concern for several of his fugitives from society in *Who Has Seen the Wind*. Here we are aware of certain similarities between the environment of the North and that of the West. Mitchell's Western fugitives, Young Ben and Saint Sammy, like Thériault's Northern fugitives, adapt to an almost equally violent and ruthless environment yet survive through their instinctive awareness of Nature. Their rebellion is against the attempts of society to rule them and it is because of these attempts that their violence erupts. The teacher aware of the glint of Young Ben's knife and of a savage gleam in his eye does not press him to conform to the patterns of behaviour she exacts from the other children, and Bent Candy is punished violently by Nature, through Saint Sammy's intervention, when he threatens to encroach on Saint Sammy's wilderness.

If controlled violence is necessary for the survival in the wilderness of those who have fled civilization, uncontrolled violence evokes a strange and sadistic response in society, particularly in individuals who feel unable to act themselves, who find themselves reluctant viewers of life's drama. Langevin and Thériault both appear to be fascinated by the response of the more passive elements in society to what they apparently regard as the glamour surrounding the violent fugitive.

In *Le temps des hommes* both the lethargic hotelkeeper, Arthur Derome, and the fat and frightened cook, Maurice, are filled with admiration for Laurier's dramatic and daring act — the murder of Gros Louis. Here is Derome's reaction:

> He was astonished....For five years Laurier had irritated him, annoyed him, bored him. He had thought him cowardly. Two deaths. Because he was jealous of his wife. He, Arthur Derome, had nothing to offer in comparison.
> Perhaps everyone had misjudged him.[6]

And of Maurice we are told:

There was almost admiration in the cook's eyes. In a few minutes he had had to revise his opinion of Laurier.[7]

Similarly Agaguk is viewed as a hero by his tribe, in fact as a hero worthy to be chosen chief, because he killed Brown and escaped punishment for his act:

> "Perhaps he killed Brown," he said. "He didn't get caught. That rid us of Ramook."
> Avenging murderer, Agaguk had not been caught! This was an exploit to recount on winter evenings. The feat of a chief.[8]

Sudden and often unpredictable acts of violence can, however, appear as weakness rather than courage. This idea is underscored most memorably in Langevin's novel when the cook discovers that killing a man is easier than cooking an omelette:

> He, Maurice, had killed and it had been easy, easier even than making an omelette, almost involuntary. There had been a sort of injustice in this ease.[9]

Only Agaguk displays real strength of character by resisting the temptation to play the public hero and by withdrawing from the limelight to a life of fulfillment with his family in his wild environment. Watching the tribal leaders, who come to beg him to be chief, walk away across the tundra he feels well-satisfied with his decision.

This ideal isolation of the strong, where violence is controlled by love and where vigor is so intense that 'a white death' is avoided, is rare in recent Canadian fiction. More often than violence, usually preceded or followed by a flight to the wilderness, is a seemingly inevitable result of futile protests against the trivialities of false-fronted towns and ugly cities and against the land itself. The Canadian environment frequently appears massive and unresponsive, dominating the individual who, frustrated and terrified, rushes lemming-like to his violent destruction.

FOOTNOTES

[1] *Agaguk*, p. 211 — in French (p. 148 — in English translation).
[2] *Le torrent*, Beauchemin, Montréal, 1950, p. 19 (translations — mine).
[3] Ibid., p. 25.
[4] Ibid., p. 46.
[5] *Agaguk*, p. 227.
[6] *Le temps des hommes*, p. 210 (translation — mine).
[7] Ibid., p. 178.
[8] *Agaguk*, p. 280.
[9] *Le temps des hommes*, p. 195.

## VII

## IN SEARCH OF NORTH: GROVE'S CANADIAN SIBERIA

Frederick Philip Grove's search for self in a northern setting was clearly basic to his maturing, first as a man and thereafter as a writer. It was his northern quest, begun in Siberia and completed years later in Western Canada (his new Siberia), which led him to self-understanding and to his best work. He readily admitted this in his autobiography:

> The effect of that (the Siberian) landscape on me was enormous and enduring; that is why I am enlarging upon it... the Steppes changed my whole view of life: the steppes got under my skin and into my blood. Life as a student in Paris, life in the various parts of the world through which I was to hurry during the years that followed, paled in my eyes whenever I thought of the steppes; and only when I struck my roots into the west of Canada did I feel at home again. In the steppes only, so it seemed, life was lived as life pure and simple, as life qua life. For here was the staggering fact: these steppes were inhabited; they were peopled by man. Perhaps, in this experience, I must look for the reason why, when stranded in America, I remained in Canada and clung to it with my soul till it had replaced Siberia as the central fact in my adult mentality.[1]

Caught up in charting the power and mystery of the vast western spaces — which he invariably viewed as essentially northern — and their effect on the imagination and on the body, Grove was the first important novelist of English Canada to base a significant number of literary creations on his perceptions of northern living. He showed that he was aware of both northern dream and northern nightmare and of the struggle which could sometimes blunt feeling altogether to produce a sordid reality. He found the struggle for survival of supreme excitement and confessed that his own insights into this struggle (both physical and spiritual) had perhaps been achieved because he had known other environments — many of them softer and more sophisticated — and by contrast had felt a strong emotional pull to this one. These emotions which Grove describes as his own in *In Search of Myself* are translated closely into those of his character Niels Lindstedt in *Settlers of the Marsh*: "... the pretty junipers of Sweden has been replaced in his affections by the more virile and fertile growth of the Canadian north. The short ardent summer and the long violent winter had captivated him: There was something heady in the quick pulse of the seasons..."[2] and "he had emigrated; and the mere fact that he was uprooted and transplanted had given him a second sight, had awakened powers of vision and sympathy in him which were far beyond his education and upbringing."[3]

Native Canadians, he said, perhaps through a lack of objectivity, often failed to grasp the implications of this struggle with the northern wilderness. In any case, Grove stressed his own belief that "Canada needed to be fought for by the soul: but very few Canadians know it."[4]

Grove too was apparently the first English-Canadian novelist to stress the similarities between Canada and Siberia — "we have the exact counterpart of almost every Siberian landscape in the west of Canada."[5] This comparison has been restated often in the last decade or two by writers as diverse in their attitudes and backgrounds as Hugh MacLennan and Brian Moore, but somewhat pedantically and without Grove's passionate associations. Grove's recognition, then, of this Siberian-Canadian analogy is simply not the fleeting academic recognition accorded this fact by most other Canadian writers, but a deep-seated feeling which reaches to the marrow of his bones. For Grove in his best work the two dominant landscapes of Western Canada (as of Siberia) the prairie grassland (the steppes) and the bush (the taiga) are the overpowering reality.

The bush-taiga is the landscape which is the backdrop for *Settlers of the Marsh* and *The Turn of the Year*, but it is the prairie-steppes as described in *Fruits of the Earth*, *Our Daily Bread*, and *The Yoke of Life* which most moved Grove and which is most important to his work. It is a landscape which he never seems to tire of describing in passages such as this:

North of that line (the Somerville Line which passed through the village of Morley)... strecthed the flat prairie, unique in America.[6] The exceedingly slight slope with which it drained north-east to the river was hardly perceptible; it amounted to less than a foot in a mile. To the casual glance, it seemed flat as a table-top. To native irregularity, whether of soil accumulation or plant growth, broke its monotony. Whatever relieved the sky-line was man's work. The only native growth was the long, slender prairie grass which in a summer breeze, gave the surface of the soil the appearance of a sheet of watered silk."[7]

\* \* \*

It is a landscape in which, to him who surrenders himself, the sense of one's life as a whole seems always present, birth and death being mere scansions in the flow of a somewhat debilitated stream of vitality.[8]

It might be best at this point to clear up any lingering doubts which the reader, should he be a stranger to the Canadian prairies, might have about the 'northern' nature of this terrain, when, in fact, it is indeed 'southern' on a map of Canada. However, even a cursory glance at latitudinal lines on the world map will disclose the fact that the southern boundaries of the Canadian prairies and the southern boundaries of Siberia lie within the same latitudes. This is a fact which Farley Mowat, another Canadian writer who lived for many years in southern Saskatchewan and in the Canadian far North and who had travelled widely in Siberia too, has stressed throughout his book *Sibir* (1970). Mowat has also made a comment which seems particularly relevant in this context. Writing from a geographical and biological point of view, Mowat states in the prologue to *Tundra* (1973) that: "The climate of the northern prairies (the tundra) is not so very different from that of their southern counterparts. Winter is longer on the tundra but not a great deal colder than on the Saskatchewan plains." And indeed a number of Grove's prairie settlers are very similar in physical stamina and temperament to Mowat's explorers. One has only to think, for instance, of Niels Lindstedt and Lars Nelson battling the blizzard at the beginning of *Settlers of the Marsh*.

The question which Grove posed concerning northern survival are clearly stated in the first chapter of *The Turn of the Year*: "Such winters (Western-Canadian ones) are memorable mostly by a peculiar kind of severity which asserts itself not so much by unusually low temperatures as by the unremitting dead level of below-zero weather which perseveres month after month....In such winters you may sometimes feel that it is an adventure of nearly overweening daring to stay in the north of this western world. Shall we survive? Or will winter, who by that time appears to us almost as a stalking enemy, win out?"[9] This may all sound rather bleak, but Grove goes on to say, in very Thoreauvian tones, that northern survival does have its special rewards. It can produce heightened perceptions and vitality: "We are not surfeited at any time with the sweets of the seasons: our appetites are kept sharp; and what we lack in the breadth of our nature-experience, we make up for in depth, in intensity. I doubt whether people in the south ever become quite such ardent lovers of even the most trivial things in nature as we do."[10]

The effects of the northern climate on the frontiersman is the question which fascinated Grove throughout his work. A successful pioneer, like a successful explorer, must enjoy a contest with a land which, to ordinary men, seems unconquerable. Even more than the explorer, who is after all nomadic, the pioneer must make his mark on the land — must, as Grove says, conquer it. He must have a physical endurance and stamina which enable him to persist and endure when other men give in or flee. Above all he must have a taste for loneliness. Clearly such men are rare. Abe Spalding, John Elliot, Mr. Amundsen and Niels Lindstedt are all variations on this type.

Ideal possibilities for the growth of the individual are presented by such an intense physical and emotional contest — possibilities of the sort envisaged by the German writer Rilke: "...but it is clear that we must hold to what is difficult; everything in Nature grows and defends itself in its own way and is characteristically and spontaneously itself, seeks at all costs to be so and against all opposition. We know little, but that we must hold to what is difficult is a certainty that will not forsake us; it is good to be solitary, for solitude is difficult; that something is difficult must be a reason the more for us to do it."[11]

Most of Grove's dominant male characters basically subscribe to this belief, but where the tragedy lies — and invariably and paradoxically in Grove's work tragedy is the lot of the 'successful' pioneer — is in the fact that solitude fails to teach them the inner self-knowledge which Rilke expects as the result of solitude. They feel the compulsion to conquer the land and, from this conquest, to reap a golden harvest. Yet Grove himself seems convinced that such a conquest is destructive.[12] Moreover — again partly it seems through his reading of Throeau,[13] Grove concludes that poverty is necessary for perception as, inevitably, a thirst for material conquest blunts feelings of every kind — feelings for the land and feelings for other human beings. Through the characters in his novels, then, Grove demonstrates Thoreau's contention that the man who tills the land for greater returns than his own immediate needs is slave rather than free man. Abe Spalding, John Elliot, and Mr. Amundsen once more are the characters who become, in varying degrees, both tyrants and victims in their materialistic exploitation of the land.

It is particularly in relationships with women that men such as these fail. For as Grove remarks in *The Search of Myself* and demonstrates throughout his work: "For the purposes of the pioneer conquest of nature certain qualities are needed in man which are imcompatible with that tender devotion which can turn the relation of the sexes into a thing of beauty."[14]

The most brutal husband among Grove's 'successful' pioneers is Mr. Amundsen of *Settlers of the Marsh*. Yearly he begets children he does not want and then forces his wife to bring about miscarriages through hard work in the fields and woods. Misery, ill-health and finally a traumatic death result. Moreover, another disastrous consequence of the Amundsen's marriage is that the daughter Ellen's whole attitude to sex is, not surprisingly, warped by her observations of her parents' married life. Consequently, she refuses to marry Niels — a man who really loves her and who has made provisions for avoiding the tragic pioneer pattern of feminine slavery for his wife. Still, Grove was obsessed with the hardship — slavery, he called it — to which most women were reduced in this new northern wilderness: "There woman is the slave, just as she is the slave in the uncivilized steppes of Siberia. A pioneering world, like the nomadic world of the steppes, is a man's world. Man stands at the centre of things; man bears the brunt of the battle: woman is relegated to the tasks of a helper. It is an unfortunate arrangement of nature that the burden of slavery, for such it is in all but name, should be biologically aggravated."[15] Examples of such slavery are everywhere in Grove's work. One thinks at once of John Elliot's daughters Gladys and Isabel (*Our Daily Bread*) after their marriages, and even of Ruth Spalding (*Fruits of the Earth*) and Mrs. Elliot (*Our Daily Bread*). Although the latter two women have much to be thankful for in the steadiness of their husbands and the physical comforts which eventually surround them, they are nevertheless unhappy and lonely woman. Mrs. Elliot only admits to this and to the gulf between her husband and herself when she realizes that she is dying and then only her eldest daughter, Gladys, in this brief conversation:

> "Gladys, I know it is a sin. I can't help it. The rest... They are all my children. But I must tell you. They are all strangers."
> "I know mother, I know. And so, at heart, is father."
> "How can you tell?"
> "Never mind, mother. He's a man."[16]

Then just before her death, Mrs. Elliot commits the only act of protest that she has committed in a lifetime. She forces Gladys to harness the horses and to drive her to a dance. A sagging and grotesque figure, Mrs. Elliot musters the strength to totter around the dance floor, and, on her return home she exclaims in pathetic satisfaction: "For once in my life I have had a good time!"[17]

It is this emotional disharmony between the sexes which is responsible for many of the bleakest passages in Grove's work. This emotional disharmony is, moreover, exaggerated by the fact that the harsh climate, while often enhancing a man's physical appearance, quickly destroys a woman's physical beauty. In *Fruits of the Earth,* for instance, Abe Spalding becomes more ruggedly handsome and distinguished looking as he ages — whereas his wife Ruth very early in their marriage loses her slenderness and fragile good looks, becoming thickset, coarse-looking and unattractive. Abe soon finds her physically repulsive. Tragically, they spend the greater part of their lives side by side, yet isolated and alienated from each other — not in Rilke's proud free loving isolation where the "two solitudes protect and border and salute each other," but in hostile separateness and lovelessness.

This aspect of Grove's northern vision, together with the pioneer's materialistic attitudes are chiefly responsible for the feeling of doom, the atmosphere of tragedy which pervades Grove's work. It is a combination which produces a northern nightmare. Yet side by side with this is Grove's awareness of the special beauty of his Canadian Siberia in every season and his perceptions of the as yet unrealized northern dream. He transmits the feeling that there is a magic quality in this environment that may yet prove regenerative for the man who, seeking to live in harmony with it, rather than striving to conquer it, may yet find both vitality and peace — for himself and for those he loves.

FOOTNOTES

1. *In Search of Myself*, Macmillan, Toronto, 1946, p. 150.
2. *Settlers of the Marsh*, McClelland and Stewart, Toronto, 1966 (first published 1925), p. 55.
3. Ibid., p. 60.
4. *In Search of Myself*, p. 150.
5. Ibid.
6. Grove seems unaware of its similarity to the arctic tundra.
7. *Fruits of the Earth*, McClelland and Stewart, Toronto, 1933, p. 135.
8. Ibid., p. 137.
9. *The Turn of the Year*, McClelland and Stewart, Toronto, 1923, p. 20.
10. *The Turn of the Year*, p. 24.
11. Rainer Maria Rilke, *Letters to a Young Poet*, Norton, New York, 1934, p. 53.

    Grove's fascination with solitude comes too from his interest in the Thoreauvian ideal of solitude. In *A Search for America* (McClelland and Stewart, Toronto, 1971 — first published 1927) Grove remarks: "I began to suspect that there might be more wisdom in this 'hermit's' mode of life than in that of the most refined and cultured shcolar (p. 260); and in *In Search of Myself* he talks of his new vision of a Thoreauvian sort of hermitage: "A nostalgia arose for a place of refuge where I might live if I ever realized that minimum income. A vision arose quite spontaneously, the moment the idea had taken shape. I would build a shack on some hillside overlooking a stream and the woods..." (p. 237).
12. This is a belief which contemporary Canadian writers — Margaret Atwood for instance in her long poem "Progressive Insanities of a Pioneer" — have stressed in recent years; but in this attitude Grove was again a pioneer in English Canadian Literature.
13. In two out of the four books which comprise *A Search for America* the captions are from Throeau and both have to do with a relinquishing of the North American materialistic standards of successful living: "The cost of a thing is the amount of what I will

call life which is required to be exchanged for it, immediately or in the long run;" and, "None can be an impartial or wise observer of human life but from the vantage ground of what we should call voluntary poverty." If we still doubt the Thoreauvian influence on Grove, Grove himself stresses this influence within the text of *A Search for America* when he states that in his opinion American Letters were "dominated by three great figures: Lincoln, Lowell, Thoreau" (p. 145): and he goes on to remark, "Where Lincoln, Lowell, Thoreau accidents? But accidents do not happen! ... Where was the soil that had borne them, so it might bear me?" (p. 146).

14 *In Search of Myself*, p. 224.
15 Ibid., pp. 223 & 224.
16 *Our Daily Bread*, Macmillan, Toronto, 1928, pp. 88 & 89.
17 Ibid., p. 131.

## VIII

## GABRIELLE ROY'S NORTHERN INNOCENTS

Innocence has always been a primary concern of Gabrielle Roy. All her central and most moving characters are essentially innocents: Rose-Anna (*Bonheur d'occasion*), Luzina (*La petite poule d'eau*) Alexandre Chenevert (*Alexandre Chenevert*), Pierre (*La montagne secrète*), Maman (*La route d'Altamont*), Deborah ("Les Satellites") and Elsa (*La rivière sans repos*). Yet gradually as her vision evolves, Roy comes to see innocence as the product of the vast, desolate and harsh Northern Canadian wilderness. It is the apparent paradox — that a soft, urban and sophisticated civilization seems to spread corruption and discontent, whereas a harsh northern wilderness can produce and preserve innocence and a measure of contentment — which increasingly grasps her imagination. It is a paradox which culminates in Roy's most recent novel on this theme, *La rivière sans repos*.

This essential conflict in Roy's fiction also arises from her concern with innocence. All her fiction depicts the conflict between simplicity and complexity,[1] between an innocent individual's search for fulfilment and happiness, and, almost invariably, his failure to escape the trap laid by contemporary civilization. Thus he frequently finds himself trapped, or, to use Roy's word, 'caged', by the pressures of society. In *La rivière sans repos* it is Thaddeus, the wise old stone-carver, who exposes this human predicament: ' "That's the whole story of man in essence," Thaddeus concluded, "just that too difficult choice between life in the great outdoors, proud and self-sufficient, or with the others, in the cage." '[2] Because of their innocence Roy's characters struggle valiantly, but for the most part ineffectually, to escape their doom. The bars on their cages become perceptibly thicker from novel to novel and the implications more sinister from the appearance of *Alexandre Chenevert*.

Earlier for instance, Luzina in *La petite poule d'eau*, though in opposition to the forces of sophistication and complexity, is nevertheless allowed by and large to win her small battles against them, chiefly because these forces penetrate only fleetingly and with difficulty into her wilderness stronghold. Certainly she does not understand the bad-tempered and frustrated teacher, Miss O'Rorke, nor the school-master whose chief interest seems to be massacring the wild life with which the Tousignant family have lived in such close harmony. Above all she finds governmental red tape incomprehensible. Nevertheless, all these alien and disconcerting intrusions on the family's wilderness tranquility are brief and do not permanently impair Luzina's placidity, good-temper, tolerance, faith and contentment.

But Alexandre Chenevert's position in life is very different from Luzina's. From the beginning of *Alexandre Chenevert* Roy makes it perfectly clear that her pathetic and naive hero is repressed and defeated through his unwillingness and inability to come to terms with his urban environment: "The city had certainly conspired to prevent him sleeping, all society against Alexandre."[3] Shut up in his teller's cage he views life through bars, and like any creature who has been caged for a long time, he is frightened when outside the cage. He glimpses a life of goodness, freedom and tranquility in his brief sojourn in Le Gardeur's wilderness cabin, but finally he feels unprepared by his past life to accept the challenge of a wilderness idyll. In his unhappy innocence he pays tribute to innocence fulfilled as he views Le Gardeur's happy life — a life which does not depend on taking from anyone else.

Pierre in *La montagne secrète* experiences conflict in some ways similar to Alexandre's. With the total commitment so typical of Roy's innocent, Pierre goes northward hoping to perfect his art and find the ideal subject. His quest is single-minded, yet because of his innocence he fears harming others he encounters. Thus he fears involvement with Nina and breaks off with her because, although he loves her, he realizes that he is in a sense married to his art and cannot therefore devote himself to her as well. Even in his relationship with the animals he encounters, his gentleness and sensitivity persist. He is, for instance, guilt-ridden during his pursuit of the cariboo for food because he is obsessed with the perception that the cariboo is closely related to him — his brother as he says — and therefore has an equal right to life. Sophistication and hardness never do come to Pierre. He remains essentially gentle and innocent. Roy makes it clear that with his attitudes he can survive, although often with difficulty, in the Northern Canadian wilderness, but that he is wholly out of step with contemporary urban patterns. There is a striking and amusing example of his inability to fall in with city ways when shortly after his arrival in Paris he shouts out a greeting to a young man canoeing on the Seine just as he would have done to a lonely stranger travelling down the MacKenzie or Churchill River.

City sophistication destroys him as it destroys Alexandre Chenevert and Deborah in "Les Satellites". Pierre finds solitude in Paris unbearable in a way that wilderness solitude was not: This Canadian wasteland, this boundless Siberia of our country — how could it indeed compare with that other solitude toward which he was winging, the utterly mysterious solitude of streets filled with people, with footsteps, and with light!"[4] Increasingly he feels caged in the city, suffocated by pressures he does not really understand:

> Then the door closed, he sat down at the foot of the bed, crossed his hands over his knees, and the sadness of soul that cities conveyed to him wound itself around him. Here the monster was full-grown. Through the small window entered flashes of neon, the glare of illuminated billboards, and a ceaseless, dreadful uproar. And then a wave of bewilderment towered high and broke over him, so appalling a wave that it took his breath away, and he felt almost swept off, even from the deepest of his memories.[5]

Deprived of what Roy, like Thoreau, clearly considers to be the barks and tonics of the wilderness, he continues to languish and at last dies in the city. Even Pierre's art has suffered by his exposure to civilization, by his 'imprisonment' far from the inspiration of his wild, secret, and for him, magic mountain.

Roy's most vulnerable innocents, however, are her Inuit innocents, those who in various ways perceive truth and make commitments to their vision of the truth — characters such as Thaddeus, Ian and particularly Elsa in *La rivière sans repos*. Like Yves Thériault's perceptive northern primitives, Ashini, Ikoué and

Tayaout, they are totally committed to the goals they undertake. They cannot compromise, a factor which is the source of their strength, but at the same time the reason for their eventual destruction because they inevitably have to cope with a 'white' society which is based on compromise.

Elsa's total devotion to her illegitimate son Jimmy, like Hester Prynne's devotion to Pearl in Hawthorne's *The Scarlet Letter*, becomes her reason for living, and no temptation makes her deviate from what she considers to be the path of duty. She deems no sacrifice too great if she can only fulfill her purpose. Hers is the complete committment of the simple and innocent imagination: "... (she) did not know what to say except that her soul was so preoccupied with him it had no room for anyone else. From morning till night since Jimmy was born, there had never been sufficient time for him."[6]

Roy show us, however, that Elsa's devotion is doomed by the forces of a soft and greedy civilization. The very fact that Jimmy is white (blue-eyed and fair-haired), born of Elsa's rape by an American G.I. stationed briefly at Fort Chimo, makes Elsa feel that she must somehow exert herself in an extraordinary way so as to give him 'white' possessions and a 'white' upbringing. She is willing to concede at first that likely white is right. Having subscribed to this idea, Elsa, Roy shows us, soon becomes for a time, like the white women of the community, an unhappy victim of Parkinson's law. From her first purchase of the pale blue nylon snowsuit from the Hudson's Bay store window, Elsa becomes involved in a frantic pursuit of acquisitions for Jimmy.

However, such sustained efforts for material possessions as those which Elsa puts forth periodically are really out of keeping with what Roy sees as the basically easy-going and happy Eskimo temperament. After working for some time for Mme Beaulieu, Elsa becomes moody and unhappy. She has learned through her own experiences, but particularly through her observations of Mme Beaulieu, that by material acquisitions an individual does not achieve happiness or freedom, but instead builds a cage for himself.

But Elsa differs from the Whites like Mme Beaulieu because she cannot collapse weakly within her cage, nor can she obscure her perception of the truth by a hedge of hypocrisy. Her dedication to

Jimmy and the honesty of her nature will not permit this. There is no compromise for Elsa. Once she comes to see civilization as bad, she decides with all the simplicity and innocence of the primitive to take Jimmy and set out for the only retreat she can think of — the wilderness of her ancestors. Hard as she knows this life to be from all the stories Winnie and Thaddeus have told, she also feels, from her understanding of these same stories, that paradoxically happiness too was a product of this life.

Taking Jimmy with her, Elsa does return to the old Fort Chimo on the other side of the river and lives with the dour but resourceful and thoughtful Uncle Ian a life which is almost totally in keeping with the ideal simplicity which she had previously vaguely imagined. Consequently Elsa feels content with her new life. Jimmy, weaned away from the baubles of civilization, is no longer a spoiled brat but a happy and lovable small boy.

Still, the old bogey of Gabrielle Roy's fiction, civilization, at last intrudes even here. When Jimmy approaches school age, the police come to warn Elsa that she must return to organized society so that Jimmy can receive a formal education. Realizing that for Jimmy and for herself such a move would be disastrous, she attempts with Ian's help to flee farther into the wilderness, but the child falls desperately ill and to save him Elsa begs Ian to return to the fort. This of course means a return to 'captivity', as Ian points out in anger and frustration: "You're like all the others," said Uncle Ian. "Made for captivity."[7] Once back at New Fort Chimo with Jimmy in hospital, Ian awaits the outcome together with Elsa. Quickly, with a series of penicillin injections, a cure is effected. But the ease of the cure seems evil to Ian who perceives its tragic implications. A devoted mother will do anything to rescue her child from death — even if it means captivity for her, and ironically for the child too, for the rest of their lives. The implication of such a discovery as penicillin, Ian realizes, is that the Whites and their society are bound to overpower the primitives and what remains of their ways: "Penicillin — that was what "they" had now, besides everything else, to trap free men."[8]

Thus throughout *La rivière sans repos* Roy continually juxtaposes two human possibilities: The primitive, hard, free and joyful versus the civilized, soft, caged and morose. Because Roy is realistic, she cannot point only to the romantic and beneficial aspects of the primitive and his habits together with the beauty of the North. She realizes that the North is also a cruel and terrifying environment: "the sterile and pitiless extent" and "the infinite misery of the Arctic" are among the expressions she uses to designate it.

Still, whatever the threatening doom of their natural environment and its alien rulers, Roy's primitives continue to live, and as long as they exist she cannot help being amused and delighted by the childlike freshness of their insights and wisdom. Their views of world affairs and of government action Roy finds particularly enchanting. When, for instance, Elsa and the ancient Eskimo woman in the old cemetery discuss Jimmy's origins, Elsa explains that his father was an American soldier who is now probably on the other side of the world. The old woman in a flash has an insight into the whole matter, yet because of her basic faith and trust in life itself, her conclusion is optimistic: "If soldiers are continually being sent far away from their homes, they're bound to get lonely and will make children to leave behind them. Thanks to war and the mixture of blood, the human race will perhaps finally be born."[9]

In the course of the same discussion the old woman tries to understand the government. She realizes that she is alive at the moment only because of her government pension. Yet what puzzles her is why the government wants to keep a person alive when he is no longer useful: "It's curious, all that. The government, which has never seen us, gives us enough to live on when we're no longer good for anything or anybody. That isn't the way to make death easier. To leave when you have enough to live forever — that's hard."[10]

Finally, in connection with the Vietnam war, Roy's innocents make a number of astute observations — perceptions as clear-sighted as a thoughtful child's. Elsa, for instance, seeing Vietnamese depicted in a newspaper, is at once aware of the similarity between the Vietnamese and the Eskimo, both in their appearances and in their predicament with regard to the Americans. When she perceives this, intuitively she is sure that her son Jimmy, emulating his father, will make love with a dusky native girl and that her grandson will thus be born on the other side of the world, for, as she notes, life repeats itself in fulfilling its strange patterns.

Such perceptions — Elsa's clearest — are a product of solitude and reverie, not of the years when she had slaved to acquire material possessions for Jimmy. She had then been obliged to conform in large measure to patterns dictated by the Whites, and during this time she began vaguely to feel that she was moving away from her true self. It is only when she no longer cares about the 'White' world and returns to the shack by the Koksoak River that she escapes its domination more completely than she had during her wilderness flight, for her escape is mental and spiritual now. Her dreams transport her for longer and longer periods into another world.

It is this ability to dream when all else fails which finally distinguishes Roy's northern innocents. For Elsa, Thaddeus and Pierre, the dream becomes the overwhelming reality since it is only through their dreams that they can escape the pace and sophistries of the modern world. This dream-reality also provides them with a self-knowledge. For Pierre, the artist, and Thaddeus, the stone-carver, their dreams and the self-knowledge they provide are the inspiration and the basis of their art. For Elsa dreams alone give her a measure of release and fulfillment — enabling her to transcend her own loneliness, the squalor of the contemporary Inuit encampment and the bleakness of the white garrison, and to establish a close primitive relationship with her natural environment, particularly with the river.

Finally, It is the mythic North which fosters this dream for Roy's northern innocents, as it does for Yves Thériault's, for it is only here, they suggest, that those endowed with special courage and perceptions may find wisdom, renewal and self-knowledge. The bleak white arctic spaces, in discouraging vigorous physical activity, seem to inspire the imagination and foster the capacity to dream.

## FOOTNOTES

1. See Albert LeBrand's essay, "Gabrielle Roy ou l'être partagé," Etudes françaises, lre année, no 2 (juin 1965) pp. 39-65, in which he discusses Roy's attempts to reconcile such opposites.
2. *La rivière sans repos*, p. 185 (*Windflower* — p. 54).
3. *Alexandre Chenevert*, p. 31.
4. *La montagne secrète*, p. 140 (*The Hidden Mountain*, p. 116).
5. Ibid., p. 151. (pp. 125 &126).
6. *La rivière sans repos*, pp. 174-175 (*Windflower* — p. 46).
7. Ibid., p. 239 (p. 94).
8. Ibid., pl 248 (p. 101).
9. Ibid., p. 226 (p. 85).
10. Ibid., p. 227 (p. 85).

## IX

## YVES THERIAULT:
## THE CONSCIENCE OF CONTEMPORARY CANADA

In part, both Thériault's imaginative vision and his moral stand stem from his link with the romantics and his endorsement of primitivism. Like the American transcendentalists, Emerson and Thoreau, and of course like the European romantics before them, Thériault is convinced that man must look to nature for his most significant lessons in living. He shows many times in such novels as *Ahinin, Le Ru d'Ikoué, Agaguk*, and *Tayaout, fils d'Agaguk* that the man who fails to respond to nature-as-teacher is doomed to emotional and spiritual sterility.

However, Thériault differs in several ways from both earlier and contemporary writers on this theme in other countries. His concern is specifically with twentieth century Canada and with the environmental difference which he finds distinguishes Canada from other industrial western nations — namely, the extensive reserves of virtually unspoiled wilderness which still remain. He explores this environmental peculiarity and calls attention to the moral responsibility which it creates for contemporary Canadians.

Before probing the most original aspects of Thériault's vision, it is also important to call attention to certain Thoreauvian attitudes to which Thériault clearly subscribes. Such famous Thoreauvian statemests as: "In Wildness is the Preservation of the World," "Simplify, simplify, simplify," and "In civilization, as in a southern latitude man degenerates at length, and yields to the incursion of more northern tribes" — are also basic to Thériault's vision, although because he is a novelist his work is not reducible to mottos. Like Thoreau too, Thériault is obsessed with North America's first inhabitants, and the important secrets which he feels they have preserved and may reveal about life's basic essences. Thoreau's thesis and Thériault's too, for instance, is that we must not seek to 'civilize' the Indian. In his unspoiled state only indigenous man can keep the balance of nature because he does not want to use up more than he needs for survival.

The point at which Thériault parts company with Throeau is over the Thoreauvian idea that the wilderness exists to revitalize a tired and decadent civlization. Thériault, writing well over a century after Thoreau, looks back over a much longer period of technological 'progress' and sees absolutely no merit in nineteenth or twentieth century civilization. Contemporary civilized man, for Thériault, is invariably degenerate man. Chiefly because of his greed and softness he is responsible for walling himself up in urban ghettos. (The 'cul-de-sac' — "une rue sans issue" — is one of Thériault's favorite urban images.) To such streets, he notes at the beginning of *Aaron*, no purifying fragrance of pine or spruce can ever penetrate.

Thériault in such novels as *Ashini*, *Agaguk*, and *Tayaout fils d'Agaguk* warns that the destructive march of civilization and technological progress into the pure northern wilderness is so far-advanced that only a miracle will save the wilderness. Thus his plea through his northern novels and his attempt to awaken our consciences before the destruction is complete. For skeptics who consider that Thériault is unnecessarily gloomy in his moral stand — in his depiction, for instance, of Ashini and Tayaout as would-be but ironically misunderstood saviours — one has only to pick up almost any newspaper or news magazine to find factual accounts of the disastrous consequences which he has been forecasting over the past decades. Thériault's insights in *Ashini* (1961) and in *Le Ru d'Ikoué* were in fact substantiated within a decade by *Time*. The caption of one 1972 article states:

> If all goes well according to Premier Robert Bourassa's preliminary plan, about 140,000 sq. mi. of Northern Quebec will be flooded or drained to marshall headwaters for the projected James Bay hydro development. To Bourassa's Liberal government, the mammoth project — which could cost as much as $10 billion and take up to ten years to build — holds the promise of 125,000 new jobs during the construction phase alone. But to the 5,000 Cree Indians who roam the wilderness as trappers and hunters, the coming of the bull-dozers will ultimately mean cultural annihilation.[1]

Of course we all know what happened here: how the warnings in fact and fiction came to nothing.

From Thériault's perspective there can be no compromise with the forces of civilization. The individual who wishes to preserve his integrity and humanity must somehow escape to the most remote wilderness where the bulldozer and the company town will not follow him. If he weakens and returns to a softer life he is undone — as Agaguk is at last in the sequel to *Agaguk, Tayaout, fils d'Agaguk*. Thériault makes it clear then that because of the harshness and perils of the Canadian wilderness, the individual who goes there in pursuit of a dream must be fully committed because invariably within the dream he has to contend with the nightmare. The northern nightmare — visible or invisible — is inevitably white, like the 'agiortok', the white wolf, in *Agaguk* or the white bear in *Tayaout, fils d'Agaguk*. Always the demon of a white death lurks. Because of the continuous struggle against almost insuperable odds, the individual, if he does 'overcome', emerges from an epic battle Canadian style as a hero — the tested, tried and proved hero of epic proportions that Agaguk becomes at the end of the novel *Agaguk*.

It is above all, however, Thériault's conception of love and sexuality in connection with social evolution and with the wilderness obsession which distinguish his vision from that of other writers — particularly North American ones. In both the nineteenth and twentieth centuries a considerable number of writers have sought the ideal relationship between man and woman. D.H. Lawrence is of course particularly notable in this century for his pursuit of the truth about human sexual relationships, and his conclusion seems to be that fulfilment in the relationships between man and woman is rare, primarily because the human social environment is wrong. Lawrence underscores the fact that the ideal and equal relationship in which the man and the woman meet like "two eagles in mid air"[2] in a "lovely state of free, proud singleness, which ... submits to the yoke and leash of love but never forfeits its own proud singleness, even while it loves and yields"[3] rarely occurs because of the constricting pressures of modern society.

In the nineteenth century such writers as Margaret Fuller (*Woman in the Nineteenth Century* — 1855), George Gissing (*The

*Odd Women* — 1893) and Nathaniel Hawthorne (*The Scarlet Letter* — 1850) also concluded that the social climate was unsatisfactory to the ecstatic and lasting sort of sexual relationship of which they caught elusive glimpses. For all these writers there is the realization that until the role of woman changes, man too is a lesser creature both spiritually and intellectually. Thus a New Woman is seen as the salvation of Man. Margaret Fuller writes:

> that the idea of Man, however imperfectly brought out, has been far more so than that of woman; that she, the other half of the same thought, the other chamber of the heart of life, needs now to take her turn in the full pulsation, and that improvement in the daughters will best aid in the reformation of the sons of this age.[4]

And one of Gissing's women states:

> There must be a new type of woman, active in every sphere of life: a new worker out in the world, a new ruler of the home. Of the old ideal virtues we can retain many, but we have to add to them those which have been thought appropriate only in men. Let a woman be gentle, but at the same time let her be strong; let her be pure of heart, but none the less wise and instructed... The mass of women have always been paltry creatures, and their paltriness has proved a curse to men. So, if you like to put it in this way, we are working for the advantage of men as well as for our own.[5]

In the light of statements such as these it is ironic that the New Woman sought after and envisaged by Fuller, Gissing, Hawthorne, Lawrence and mid-twentieth writers as well, emerges in the contemporary northern Canadian wilderness as an untutored Eskimo woman — strong and gentle, pure of heart, yet deeply wise and able to hold her own in a man's world — and it is clearly because of her that Agaguk attains both peace and heroism.

Nevertheless, Thériault makes it apparent that the relationship of Iriook and Agaguk is only possible because of their wilderness environment. Other couples Thériault introduces us to appear at first equally blessed by compatibility — Pippo and his wife in *Amour au goût de mer* and Aaron and Viedna in *Aaron*. But Thériault shows that they are doomed — doomed ultimately by their urban environment. Fabien and Edith in *La fille laide* have a deeper relationship, chiefly because they live in the country, but they too cannot escape far enough from existing social patterns.

Civilized society with its frivolous and transitory fashions is no setting, Thériault indicates, for a deep and basic relationship. He is particularly critical of superficially alluring women, like Bernadette in *La fille laide*, who prove empty behind the mask of their beauty. Always warning against trite and superficial judgements, Thériault shows us that it is Edith, 'la fille laide', who possesses the essential femininity. Speaking for Thériault, Fabien persuades Edith of the basic truth of his statement that "Being beautiful is not the important thing; being womanly is."[6]

Still it is Iriook who is the complete woman — although ironically Thériault implies that she would not even draw a second glance from a 'civilized' contemporary urban male. She is nonetheless the embodiment of a male dream. Responding completely to the sexual act, faithful, courageous, vital, a devoted mate and mother, she also possesses an intuitive feminine perception and wisdom which is often shown as a complement to and check on Agaguk's sometimes foolhardy bravery and his aggressively destructive male impulses. Together they fulfil and improve each other with primitive vitality.

Love is the basis of Iriook's and Agaguk's life together. Yet, chiefly because of the wilderness setting in which it flourishes, it is a violent as well as a tender emotion. Violence, in fact, must be considered crucial to Thériault's vision. Thériault at once makes it apparent that the wilderness provides not only a sanctuary for love, but also a series of trials to test its strength and endurance. The violence of these trials proves the courage of those who can endure and survive them. For this reason Thériault sees violence not only as a significant fact of life but even as a beneficial one.

Iriook's and Agaguk's love on the tundra begins as an exhausting but satisfying animal passion. The violence of their passion alerts all their senses, paradoxically bringing to life delicate and hitherto undiscovered subtleties and loyalties. Thus Thériault considers that a sexual experience of this sort is a form of rebirth. Agaguk, for instance, decides that the accepted Eskimo custom of lending one's wife to friends on special occasions will not work for him. It happens because Iriook has totally grasped his imagination that physically he cannot bear to take another woman or to lend Iriook. Iriook, he concludes in opposition to tribal customs, must be for him alone.

Such a development of an emotional-intellectual decision from a violent physical response happens many times to Agaguk in the course of the novel. Agaguk, for instance, although at the height of his masculine strength and assertiveness, learns on a number of occasions, as after the birth of their daughter, to allow Iriook's decision to stand. He does this with difficulty — against all traditional practices again — because he is forced to realize that he must let Iriook develop as a strong individual too or he will destroy the special nature of their relationship. However, for Agaguk such decisions are painfully achieved: his emotions, Thériault shows, are tested and finally purified in the fires of violence.

Thériault obviously believes that the violence of Iriook's and Agaguk's life lends the spice of their vitality and love. Because they live so near to death and destruction in its many forms and because they both face frightful perils daily — in the snows, on the ice, in lonely hunting expeditions, from the white wolf, from unfriendly tribesmen — they are, paradoxically always deeply conscious of the power of life. With their vitality always at white heat and their courage always being proved, their admiration and consequently their love for each other increases as they struggle to preserve themselves and each other in their formidable environment.

Finally, Thériault's vision extends to art. Art, like love, Thériault believes, flourishes in its most honest, most spiritual and consequently most intense form in the wilderness, remote from the fads and mercenary motives of civilized societies which often, he feels, prevent the fulfilment of its deepest meaning and purpose. Thériault is concerned with this thesis briefly in *Agaguk* and more specifically in *Tayaout, fils d'Agaguk*. Art inspires the individual with the capacity to dream and thence to conquer brutality and acquire self-knowledge.

Tayaout, Agaguk's son, seeks to save himself and his people by his rediscovery of the symbolic green stone which in former generations had held such significance for his people. Finding the stone and removing it to the Eskimo settlement is in itself an incredibly difficult undertaking. But the significance that Tayaout assigns to the stone is immense. Its proper use, he is convinced, could mean salvation for his people. Thus he sets himself and each individual of his tribe the task of interpreting dreams and memories in stone so as to bring out, Thériault says, the 'soul' in the stone. The Eskimos, inspired by Tayaout's sincerity and courage, succeed beyond their wildest hopes and begin through their achievement to acquire self-respect. But this is short-lived. During one of Tayaout's absences to replenish the stock of stone, the others agree to sell their work to a white trader who of course will remove it to the 'decadent' south. When sculpting becomes a commercial venture and the figures fall into the hands of those who cannot comprehend the creators, their culture or inspiration, Thériault, like his hero Tayaout washes his hands of the whole undertaking. Tayaout soon perishes, like Ashini, without completing his mission of saviour to his people, because the rest of the tribe lack his strength and moral fibre.

Thus, through his studies of sensitive and perceptive characters engaged in the individualistic quests — quests which frequently take them into the northern Canadian wilderness — Yves Thériault explores such contemporary issues as the function of the wilderness in a twentieth century context, the necessity of solitude for self-knowledge, and the role of love and art in the regeneration and expansion of human perceptions. Above all, Thériault seems concerned that we stop short in our head-long pursuit of material goals and examine the position of contemporary man — before all opportunities for choice and for heroism vanish with the impending destruction of the wilderness.

FOOTNOTES

1. *Time*, April 24, 1972, pp. 12-15.
2. D.H. Lawrence, *Aaron's Rod*, New York, 1961, p. 163.
3. D.H. Lawrence, *Women in Love*, New York, 1960, p. 247.
4. Margaret Fuller, *Woman in the Nineteenth Century*, New York, 1971, pp. 23 & 24.
5. George Gissing, *The Odd Women*, New York, 1971, pp. 136 & 137.
6. *La fille laide*, Les Editions de l'Homme, 1965, p. 63.

## X

## MARGARET ATWOOD: WOMAN IN THE NORTH

Go North young woman, go North! A changed slogan. Well, of course! Times have changed!

In *Surfacing* Margaret Atwood's female protagonist launches and motivates the northern quest which triggers the action and the response of the other characters in the novel. She is the first woman character in contemporary Canadian fiction to precipitate a northern venture and to hold the reins of the undertaking. Her flight from civilization to wilderness cabin seems at first more typical of French than of English Canadian fiction.

It is fitting then that Margaret Atwood, having chosen a subject more clearly in the tradition of French Canada than of English Canada, should also set her novel in northern Quebec. She aligns herself still more closely with the French-Canadian outlook by lashing out violently — like Langevin in *L'Elan d'Amérique*, Thériault in *Ashini* and *Tayaout, fils d' Agaguk* and Roy in *La rivière sans repos* — against southern, though particularly American influences. This is evident from the first page of *Surfacing* when Atwood's protagonist sets the mood and establishes her loyalties by pointing out that even the birches are suffering from a cancerous southern blight which is spreading steadily northward. More serious evidences of the creeping southern blight are recorded as the protagonist and her friends travel northward; the American army camp, tolerated because it is "good for business"; the stuffed moose family at the filling station, dressed in human garb and waving an American flag; the fisherman, again with an American flag emblazoned on their boat, who kill because of a muderous blood lust; the clubman who wants to buy the island....After cataloguing these various separate menaces, Atwood ends by calling the Americans the "pervasive menace" to Canadian society. Again like Thériault, Langevin and Horwood — and of course like Grey Owl and Thoreau before that — Atwood suggests that the only cure for this sickness of civilization is to let the wilderness in and to emulate the Indian, for "the Indians did not own salvation but they had once known where it lived and their signs marked the sacred places, the places where you could learn the truth."[1]

However, despite her place in this tradition, Margaret Atwood is very much herself, and she quickly separates herself from all traditions when she launches a woman into the northern wilderness — a woman too who at length takes a determined stand for survival which is individual and feminine. She refuses to be a victim.

Atwood was also concerned with this theme of individual, and particularly feminine, survival and victimization in her first novel, *The Edible Woman* (1969), but in *Surfacing*, because of the northern wilderness setting, the protagonist's stance is more surprising and courageous than one might at first think. Traditionally women have survived on the frontier as either wives or prostitutes — and therefore as followers, certainly not as trail-blazers. Grove has made this point clearly and well in *In Search of Myself* when he compares the position of woman at the northern fringes of civilization with that of a slave.[2]

Atwood's persona fights against this position of slave — or, as she calls it, victim — for women, or for one individual woman anyway. She has already occupied the position of slave or victim in the city, where she has only just survived a series of soul and body-numbing events, particularly an unhappy affair with a married man and an abortion. Retreat, at least temporarily, to the northern wilderness seems in order to heal the wounds and replenish the vitality which had been almost extinguished since her wilderness childhood.

The wild island with its Thoreauvian cabin does not at first seem to provide either tranquility or freedom — chiefly because the Atwood persona now finds herself responsible for three people who are, as she proclaims desperately, "More than halfway to machine." Bored without television and edgy because of the silence, they are almost totally unresponsive to the surrounding natural environment — for as Margaret Atwood has remarked in one of her poems in *The Journals of Susanna Moodie* —

> Whether the wilderness is
> real or not
> depends on who lives there

Leadership is thus thrust upon Atwood's protagonist because she alone knows how to cope: how to chop wood, how to find her way in the forest, how to paddle a canoe and how to cook out of doors. Her unresponsive charges only come to life, if it can be called that, when the natural environment has been victimized or brutalized — as when they come upon the heron, senselessly killed and hanging from a tree on the portage. This, they feel, will make a splendid camera shot.

After several days of trying to guide this perverse and troublesome trio through the wilderness, the Atwood persona is understandably clear about one thing — she does not want to be at all like them. Consequently she becomes determined to slough off the unnaturalness, the inability to feel which has come upon her in the city, and to be again the natural woman. She finally concludes, "I tried for all those years to be civilized, but I'm not and I'm through pretending." But this is easier said than done. What good to be Anahareo without Grey Owl for mate? The 'civilized' men of Atwood's protagonist's life have brought only disaster to her.

Nevertheless, Atwood blames the modern woman too for being a victim. She would clearly subscribe to D.H. Lawrence's stand on the joint responsibility for disaster made possible by the complementary actions of the victor and the victim — for as Lawrence asserts "for every murderer there is a murderee" and "no man is robbed against his will." Thus women, Atwood shows, are frequently provocative as victims, calling out masculine brutality. This is demonstrated through the relationship between Anna and David as Atwood lays bare their shoddy marriage.

There is no doubt that Anna is the victim of David's brutal actions — such as pulling off her clothes on the pier so that he and Joe can photograph her — and his continuous perverse and obscene comments which are designed to embarass and frustrate her. Still, we find it increasingly difficult as the characters' actions and relationships are unveiled, to find Anna a sympathetic character.

She is too dishonest, too superficial. The masks she wears to hide from David — and from herself as well — together with her shirking of mature or thoughtful judgements make her, one feels at length, almost deserving of so selfish and shallow a husband as David.

Through her depiction of Anna too, Atwood is calling attention to the failure of modern pills and cosmetics to produce a more free and beautiful woman. Despite the claims of modern advertising, she shows that they contribute only ugliness and superficiality, facts which may perhaps be disguised, at least partly, under city lights, but which stand out in glaring and appalling clarity in the clear, cold northern sunlight.

In reaction to women like Anna and in a desperate attempt to become a feeling and 'natural' woman, the Atwood persona decides that she must first have a child conceived under the northern spruces, outside what she considers to be the legal and social hypocrisy and bondage of a modern marriage such as Anna's and David's, and born naturally — not torn from her anaesthetized body by forceps. Joe, simply because he happens to be her companion it seems, and also because he is a man still capable of some feeling in his own bumbling way, is to father this child. Then she will desert him, thus reversing the traditional masculine-feminine roles as she sees them, and asserting her freedom in this way. (This is a subject Atwood has already touched on in *The Edible Woman* when Ainsley decides that she needs to have a baby but not a husband because "every woman should have at least one baby....It fulfills your deepest femininity.") However, in this attempted reversal of sexual roles, the woman finds as many complications and surprises as man has traditionally found. In the end, it is hard to get along without a mate — a conclusion which both Ainsley and the protagonist of *Surfacing* reach.

If this seems a mundane conclusion for such a rebel in the sexual battle to arrive at, the protagonist nevertheless hardly lapses into a complacently conventional role. Her northern experience has been responsible for her rebirth. Her final assertion is that she will retain her new wild and natural identity, but must return to live in civilization because "withdrawing is no longer possible and the alternative is death." She will not settle for death. With her last breath she asserts her intention to be herself ... to survive ... and to avoid being a victim. It is presumably the northern wilderness which has provided her with the 'barks' and 'tonics' which she hopes will guard her from the viruses of contemporary civilization.

FOOTNOTES

[1] *Surfacing*, McClelland and Stewart, Toronto, 1972, p. 145.
[2] *In Search of Myself*, Macmillan, Toronto, 1946, pp. 223 and 224 (See quotation 15 of Chapter VII).

# INDEX

Anahareo 97
Atwood, Margaret 9-12, 13n., 17, 20, 24, 26, 28, 72, 95-99

Baffin Island 48
Belaney, Archie. *See* Grey Owl
Bernard, Harry 11, 21n.
Blais, Marie-Claire 40n., 53, 56, 58
Bodsworth, Fred 24-28
Buckler, Ernest 11, 54
Buell, John 54, 58

Cambridge Bay 50n.
Carrier, Roch 43
Churchill 47, 48
Churchill River 77
Conrad, Joseph 49, 53
Cumberland Sound 50n.

Davies, Robertson 9, 13n., 40n., 43
Dickson, Lovat 13n., 14n.
Dostoevsky, Fyodor 20, 56

Emerson, Ralph Waldo 11, 14n., 40n., 85

Fort Chimo 20, 47, 78, 79
Fort Renunciation 47
Frobisher Bay 47
Frye, Northrop 43
Fuller, Margaret 87, 88, 92n.

Gissing, George 87, 88, 92n.
Grey Owl 10-12, 14n., 24, 26-28, 30, 35, 95, 97
Grove, Frederick Philip 9, 11, 13n., 65-73

Harlow, Robert   21n.
Hawthorne, Nathaniel   78, 88
Hébert, Anne   54, 56, 57
Horwood, Harold   9-12, 17-19, 21n., 29, 35, 36, 46, 47, 95
Houston, James   47, 48
Huxley, Aldous   37

Jasmin, Claude   17

Kreisel, Henry   10, 17, 20, 21n., 40n.
Kroetsch, Robert   9, 10, 12, 35

Langevin, André   9-12, 14n., 18, 21n., 24, 25, 28, 34, 40n., 43, 53, 55, 58-61, 95
Laurence, Margaret   40n., 43
Lawrence, D.H.   55-57, 60, 87, 88, 92n., 97
LeBrand, Albert   82n.
Lemelin, Roger   21n.
Lowry, Malcolm   43

Mackenzie River   77
MacLennan, Hugh   9, 12, 13n., 14n., 40n., 43, 54, 57-59, 66
McCourt, Edward   55
Melville, Herman   53, 60
Mitchell, W.O.   61
Moore, Brian   9, 13n., 66
Mowat, Farley   13n., 24-27, 67

Newlove, John 23, 24

Orwell, George   17

Pangnirtung   44, 50n.
Pellerin, Jean   54
Pryde, Duncan   13n.

Rankin Inlet   44
Richardson, Boyce   49

Richler, Mordicai   48
Rilke, Rainer Maria   68, 69, 71, 72n.
Ross, Sinclair   18, 40n., 43, 54, 57-59
Roy, Gabrielle   9-11, 13n., 17, 18, 20, 23-25, 28, 29, 34, 35, 43, 47-49, 55, 75-82, 95

Saint-Exupéry, Antoine de   19
Salinger, J.D.   58
Schultz-Lorentzen, Finn   29, 44, 45, 48, 50n.
Siberia   9, 13, 45, 65-67, 70, 71, 77
Solzhenitsyn, Aleksandr   45

Thiériault, Yves   9-12, 17-19, 24, 27-29, 33, 34, 36-38, 43, 46, 48, 49, 50n., 54, 55, 58-61, 77, 81, 85-92, 95
Thoreau, Henry David   11, 14n., 19, 24, 28-30, 39, 68, 69, 72, 73, 77, 85, 86, 95, 96
Tolstoy, Leo   56

Ungava Bay   18

Vac, Bertrand   21n.
Voltaire, François M.A.   56

Warwick, Jack   13n.
Whitman, Walt   14n., 36
Wilson, Ethel   21n.

Yellowknife   46
York, Thomas   29, 46, 50n.